THE AUSTRALIAN
Women's Weekly
mince it

acp books

contents

The oven temperatures in this book are for conventional ovens; if you have a fan-forced oven decrease the temperature by 10-20 degrees.

minced meat

beef mince

It's almost impossible to ruin minced beef during the cooking process; sometimes the resulting sauce, rissole, meatloaf or whatever is wonderful – rich in flavour, a great colour and just the right consistency, other times it's okay, not wonderful – but always acceptable. Minced beef is liked by just about everyone – it's easy to eat for the young, the elderly and everyone in-between, it's an economical buy, and can be extended easily with a wide variety of other ingredients to make it go even further when the budget is stretched.

Once upon a time, mince was mince and it was predominantly beef – the buyer was stuck with whatever the butcher wanted to mince then sell – but now we have many choices. The least expensive mince will almost always have the highest fat content (there are exceptions – think mince made from high-quality marbled beef) and the most expensive mince will have the lowest fat content. Also available is mince derived from special breeds of cattle that might be fed on either grain or grass; all this information should be available from the butcher or on the packaging in the supermarkets. This readily available information means we can make our choices on the source and fat content of the mince – often an important issue in terms of choosing an ingredient that is best for our health and well being. There is a down-side to using super-lean mince: fat (and oil) holds and emphasises flavours and also helps break up the solid protein in the meat. This is especially noticeable during the browning and stirring of mince when making a mince sauce; the lack of fat is why the mince "clumps". Add a little oil, squash the "clumps" with a fork or potato masher then continue. Next time when making a meat sauce, buy a slightly less-lean minced beef, or add some oil.

lamb mince

Minced lamb is tasty and easy to cook with, mostly because it's quite high in fat and easily takes on the flavour of added ingredients. It's used widely in Middle Eastern, Greek and North African cuisines, although we're rapidly adopting and adapting recipes from these countries and making them our own.

pork & veal mince

Minced pork is often quite high in its fat content, making it a delight to cook with. Try using it next time you make a meat sauce for "spag bol". Like lamb, it accepts and holds added flavours well. Veal mince is usually low in fat, and is often sold combined with pork mince so that the virtues of each complement each other.

chicken & turkey mince

Chicken mince is gaining in popularity, and children love its texture and flavour. It readily takes on flavours, particularly those of Asian ingredients. Turkey mince has a great flavour and texture too; for a change, try substituting it for beef mince the next time you make a meat sauce.

sausage mince & sausages

Where would a barbecue be without sausages? Throughout this book we've included great recipes for the most readily available types – beef, lamb, pork and chicken. Apart from the regular sausages, there is a vast array of exotic sausages available in delis, butchers, supermarkets and specialty food stores. If a recipe calls for sausage mince and none is available, buy the appropriate sausage, the same weight will do – and simply squeeze the mince from the skins. A good mix for most recipes that call for sausage mince is equal quantities of beef and pork.

'spag bol'

During the last 30 years or so, spaghetti bolognese has become our national dish, it's the most eaten meal in this country. The fact that the meat sauce we affectionately call "spag bol" bears little resemblance to the traditional Italian recipe from the region of Bologna doesn't bother us at all. People claim to have discovered the magic ingredient for the best-ever sauce. From what we hear, these ingredients include barbecue sauce, fish sauce, tomato sauce (a personal favourite), tomato ketchup, soy sauce, Vegemite, Bonox, dried tomato soup mix, canned tomato soup and so on. Whatever the magic ingredient is, you can be sure that each time you make a meat sauce it will be different from the last time, but everybody will love it.

chicken & turkey

chicken, spinach and ricotta cannelloni

60g (2 ounces) baby spinach leaves, shredded finely
2 cups (500ml) bottled tomato pasta sauce
375g (12 ounces) minced (ground) chicken
⅔ cup (160g) ricotta cheese
2 tablespoons coarsely chopped fresh oregano
⅔ cup (50g) coarsely grated parmesan cheese
10 dried cannelloni tubes (100g)
¾ cup (75g) coarsely grated mozzarella cheese
2 tablespoons coarsely chopped fresh
   flat-leaf parsley

1 Preheat oven to 200°C/400°F. Grease 20cm x 30cm (8 inch x 12 inch) ovenproof dish.
2 Boil, steam or microwave spinach until wilted; rinse under cold water, squeeze excess water from spinach, chop finely.

3 Pour half the pasta sauce into dish. Combine chicken, spinach, ricotta, oregano and half the parmesan in medium bowl; season. Fill cannelloni tubes with chicken mixture; place, in a single layer, in dish. Spoon over remaining pasta sauce. Sprinkle with mozzarella and remaining parmesan. Bake, covered, about 45 minutes or until pasta is tender. Stand 10 minutes. Sprinkle with parsley to serve.
prep + cook time 1 hour 10 minutes **serves** 4
nutritional count per serving 21.7g total fat (10.6g saturated fat); 2015kJ (482 cal); 32.3g carbohydrate; 37.2g protein; 4.2g fibre
Serve with a green salad.
A piping (pastry) bag filled with the chicken mixture will make filling the cannelloni tubes really easy.

chicken meatball noodle stir-fry

500g (1 pound) thin hokkien noodles
625g (1¼ pounds) minced (ground) chicken
2 green onions (scallions), sliced thinly
1 cup coarsely chopped fresh coriander (cilantro)
2 fresh long red chillies, sliced thinly
½ cup (35g) stale breadcrumbs
1 tablespoon vegetable oil
1 bunch gai lan, chopped coarsely
¼ cup (60ml) oyster sauce
2 tablespoons sweet chilli sauce
½ cup coarsely chopped fresh mint

1 Place noodles in large heatproof bowl, cover with boiling water; separate with fork, drain.
2 Combine chicken, onion, half the coriander, half the chilli and breadcrumbs in medium bowl; season. Roll tablespoons of mixture into balls.
3 Heat wok, add oil; stir-fry meatballs, in batches, until cooked through. Remove from pan. Add gai lan; stir-fry 2 minutes or until tender.
4 Return meatballs to wok with noodles and sauces; stir-fry until noodles are heated through. Sprinkle with mint and remaining coriander and chilli.
prep + cook time 30 minutes **serves** 4
nutritional count per serving 19.2g total fat
(4.7g saturated fat); 2855kJ (683 cal);
77.8g carbohydrate; 45g protein; 5.5g fibre

spicy chicken tacos

1 tablespoon olive oil
1 medium brown onion (150g), chopped finely
500g (1 pound) minced (ground) chicken
35g (1 ounce) packet taco seasoning mix
375g (12 ounces) bottled thick and chunky
  taco sauce
½ cup (125ml) water
10 (140g) stand'n'stuff taco shells
1 cup finely shredded iceberg lettuce
1 medium carrot (120g), coarsely grated
125g (4 ounces) cherry tomatoes, quartered
½ cup (60g) coarsely grated cheddar cheese
½ cup loosely packed fresh coriander
  (cilantro) leaves
⅓ cup (80g) sour cream

1 Heat oil in large frying pan, add onion; cook, stirring, until softened. Add chicken; cook, stirring, until browned. Add taco seasoning, cook, stirring, until fragrant. Add half the taco sauce and the water; cook, stirring occasionally, about 7 minutes or until mixture thickens. Remove from heat.
2 Meanwhile, heat taco shells according to directions on packet.
3 Divide chicken mixture into shells; top with lettuce, carrot, tomato, cheese, coriander and remaining sauce. Serve topped with sour cream.
prep + cook time 25 minutes **makes** 10
nutritional count per taco 35.9g total fat
(13.3g saturated fat); 2445kJ (585 cal);
29.7g carbohydrate; 33.2g protein; 6.7g fibre
To add extra heat, serve some pickled jalapeño chillies with the tacos.

chicken kofta with tomato salad and tzatziki

625g (1¼ pounds) minced (ground) chicken
1 small brown onion (80g), chopped finely
2 cloves garlic, crushed
2 teaspoons ground cumin
2 teaspoons ground coriander
¾ cup (85g) packaged breadcrumbs
½ cup coarsely chopped fresh coriander
  (cilantro) leaves
1 tablespoon vegetable oil
2 teaspoons red wine vinegar
3 medium tomatoes (450g), cut into wedges
1 small red onion (100g), sliced thinly
¼ cup small fresh mint leaves
1 cup (250g) tzatziki

1 To make chicken kofta, combine chicken, brown onion, garlic, cumin, ground coriander, breadcrumbs and fresh coriander in medium bowl; season. Shape ¼-cups of mixture around 12 metal skewers to make sausage shapes. Place kofta on tray, cover; refrigerate 10 minutes.
2 Meanwhile, combine oil, vinegar, tomato, red onion and mint in medium bowl; season to taste.
3 Cook kofta on heated oiled grill plate (or grill or barbecue) about 15 minutes or until browned all over and cooked through.
4 Serve kofta with tomato salad and tzatziki, and warm crusty bread if you like.
prep + cook time 35 minutes **serves** 4
nutritional count per serving 25.1g total fat (7.1g saturated fat); 1973kJ (472 cal); 19.6g carbohydrate; 39.4g protein; 5.4g fibre

Tzatziki is a Greek yogurt dip made with cucumber, garlic and sometimes chopped fresh mint. You can buy tzatziki ready-made in supermarkets and delicatessens.
If using bamboo skewers, soak them in cold water for at least 30 minutes before using to prevent them from scorching during cooking.

chicken larb

1 tablespoon peanut oil
625g (1¼ pounds) minced (ground) chicken
2 cloves garlic, crushed
5cm (1 inch) piece fresh ginger (20g), grated
2 tablespoons grated palm sugar
2 tablespoons fish sauce
4 kaffir lime leaves, shredded finely
¼ cup (60ml) lime juice
¼ cup (35g) chopped roasted unsalted peanuts
1 cup loosely packed fresh coriander
   (cilantro) leaves
½ cup loosely packed fresh mint leaves
8 iceberg lettuce leaves
1 fresh long red chilli, sliced thinly

1 Heat oil in wok; stir-fry chicken until browned lightly. Add garlic and ginger; stir-fry until fragrant.
2 Add sugar, sauce and lime leaves to wok; stir-fry about 2 minutes or until chicken is coated.
3 Stir in juice and two-thirds of the peanuts, coriander and mint. Remove from heat. Spoon chicken mixture into lettuce leaves. Top with remaining peanuts, coriander and mint. Sprinkle with chilli; serve with lime wedges.

prep + cook time 30 minutes **serves** 4
nutritional count per serving 21.6g total fat (5.2g saturated fat); 1547kJ (370 cal); 8.72g carbohydrate; 34g protein; 3g fibre

hoisin turkey rice paper rolls

375g (12 ounces) minced (ground) turkey
2cm (¾ inch) piece fresh ginger (10g), grated
⅓ cup (80ml) hoisin sauce
¼ cup (60ml) sweet chilli sauce
12 x 22cm (9 inch) rice paper rounds
1 lebanese cucumber (130g), seeded, cut
   into matchsticks
1 cup (80g) bean sprouts, trimmed
75g (2½ ounces) snow peas, trimmed, sliced thinly
12 large fresh mint leaves
12 fresh coriander (cilantro) sprigs

1 Heat oiled large frying pan, add turkey and ginger; cook, stirring, until mince changes colour. Remove from heat. Stir in half the hoisin sauce and 1 tablespoon of the sweet chilli sauce.

2 Dip one sheet of rice paper in medium bowl of warm water until barely soft. Carefully lift sheet from water; place on board covered with tea towel. Spread a heaped tablespoon of turkey mixture along centre of sheet then top with some of the cucumber, sprouts, peas, mint and coriander. Roll rice paper over filling, fold in sides then roll up to enclose filling. Repeat with remaining rice paper, turkey mixture, vegetables and herbs.

3 Combine remaining sauces with about 1 tablespoon water in small bowl. Serve rolls with dipping sauce.

prep + cook time 30 minutes **makes** 12
nutritional count per roll 2g total fat
(0.4g saturated fat); 359kJ (86 cal);
8.6g carbohydrate; 7.4g protein; 1.8g fibre

Use smaller rice paper rounds for finger-food sized rolls. You can use chicken mince instead of turkey, if you like.

turkey burgers with cranberry onions

1 tablespoon olive oil
1 large red onion (300g), sliced thinly
2 tablespoons red wine vinegar
1 tablespoon brown sugar
2 tablespoons cranberry sauce
375g (12 ounces) minced (ground) turkey
3 green onions (scallions), chopped finely
⅓ cup coarsely chopped fresh flat-leaf parsley
4 bread rolls, halved
8 oak leaf lettuce leaves
1 medium tomato (150g), sliced
4 slices (80g) swiss cheese

1 To make cranberry onions, heat oil in medium frying pan, add red onion; cook, stirring occasionally, over medium heat, about 15 minutes or until onion is soft. Add vinegar and sugar; cook, stirring, 5 minutes or until caramelised. Stir in sauce; remove from heat.
2 Meanwhile, combine turkey, green onion and parsley in medium bowl; season. Shape mixture into 4 patties.
3 Cook patties on heated oiled grill plate (or grill or barbecue) about 12 minutes or until cooked through. Transfer to a plate; cover to keep warm.
4 Toast rolls, cut-side down, on grill plate until browned lightly. Sandwich lettuce, tomato, patties, cheese and cranberry onions between rolls.
prep + cook time 35 minutes **serves** 4
nutritional count per serving 16.6g total fat (5.7g saturated fat); 1839kJ (440 cal); 39.4g carbohydrate; 30.8g protein; 3.9g fibre

turkey and cranberry meatloaf

10 slices prosciutto (150g)
1 medium brown onion (150g), grated
2 green onions (scallions), sliced thinly
2 cloves garlic, crushed
750g (1½ pounds) minced (ground) turkey
2 tablespoons tomato sauce
1 tablespoon worcestershire sauce
1 egg yolk
½ cup (35g) stale breadcrumbs
⅓ cup finely finely chopped fresh flat-leaf parsley
½ cup (160g) cranberry sauce
2 tablespoons orange juice

1 Preheat oven to 200°C/400°F.
2 Grease 15cm x 20cm (6 inch x 8 inch) loaf pan. Line base and sides of pan with prosciutto, leaving overhang on long sides of pan to cover the top of the meatloaf.
3 Combine onions, garlic, turkey, sauces, egg yolk, breadcrumbs and parsley in large bowl; season. Press into pan. Fold prosciutto over to cover turkey mixture. Place pan on oven tray. Bake 45 minutes.
4 Meanwhile, combine cranberry sauce and juice in small bowl.
5 Remove meatloaf from oven; drain juices from pan. Carefully invert meatloaf onto wire rack. Place rack over oven tray. Brush meatloaf with cranberry mixture; return to oven, bake about 15 minutes or until browned and cooked through.
prep + cook time 1 hour 20 minutes **serves** 4
nutritional count per serving 12.2g total fat (3.4g saturated fat); 1760kJ (421 cal); 28.8g carbohydrate; 47.7g protein; 1.7g fibre

Serve with steamed vegetables or salad.
We used cranberry sauce not whole berry sauce.
Use chicken mince if you prefer.

red chicken meatball curry

2 teaspoons vegetable oil
1 medium brown onion (150g), chopped finely
2 cloves garlic, crushed
¼ cup (75g) thai red curry paste
500ml (2 cups) coconut milk
½ cup (125ml) water
2 kaffir lime leaves
155g (5 ounces) green beans, trimmed, halved
155g (5 ounces) oyster mushrooms, halved
1 fresh long red chilli, sliced thinly
½ cup loosely packed fresh coriander
  (cilantro) leaves
CHICKEN MEATBALLS
500g (1 pound) minced (ground) chicken
2 green onions (scallions), sliced finely
5cm (1 inch) piece fresh ginger (20g), grated
½ cup (35g) stale breadcrumbs

1 Make chicken meatballs.
2 Heat oil in large saucepan, add onion; cook, stirring, until browned lightly. Add garlic and curry paste; stir until fragrant. Add coconut milk, the water, lime leaves and meatballs; simmer, uncovered, about 10 minutes or until meatballs are almost cooked through. Add beans and mushrooms; simmer, covered, about 5 minutes or until vegetables are tender and meatballs are cooked through, season to taste.
3 Just before serving, sprinkle with chilli and coriander.
chicken meatballs Combine ingredients in medium bowl; season. Roll rounded tablespoons of mixture into balls.

prep + cook time 35 minutes **serves** 4
nutritional count per serving 44.8g total fat (26.7g saturated fat); 2533kJ (606 cal); 16.1g carbohydrate; 31.6g protein; 8.6g fibre
Serve with steamed jasmine rice.

chicken and fennel pies

1 tablespoon olive oil
1 medium brown onion (150g), sliced thinly
1 baby fennel bulb (130g), sliced thinly
500g (1 pound) minced (ground) chicken
¼ cup (35g) plain (all-purpose) flour
1½ cups (375ml) chicken stock
1 medium potato (200g), cut into 1cm (½ inch) dice
2 tablespoons finely chopped fresh flat-leaf parsley
2 sheets ready-rolled shortcrust pastry,
  halved diagonally
1 sheet ready-rolled puff pastry, quartered
1 egg yolk
½ teaspoon fennel seeds

1 Heat oil in large saucepan, add onion and fennel; cook, stirring, until soft. Add chicken; cook, stirring, until chicken is cooked through. Add flour; stir until bubbling. Gradually stir in stock. Add potato; cook, stirring occasionally, about 10 minutes or until potato is tender and mixture thickens. Remove from heat. Stir in parsley; season to taste. Cool 30 minutes.
2 Preheat oven to 200°C/400°F.
3 Grease four 1-cup (250ml) pie dishes. Line base and side of each dish with shortcrust pastry; trim edges. Divide chicken mixture into pastry cases, top with puff pastry; trim edges. Brush with egg yolk and sprinkle with seeds. Place dishes on oven tray.
4 Bake pies about 45 minutes or until browned. Stand 10 minutes before serving.

prep + cook time 1 hour 20 minutes (+ cooling)
makes 4
nutritional count per pie 28.1g total fat (10.3g saturated fat); 2161kJ (517 cal); 33.6g carbohydrate; 31.2g protein; 2.9g fibre

warm chicken and crisp wonton salad

2 teaspoons peanut oil
500g (1 pound) minced (ground) chicken
1 tablespoon grated palm sugar
5cm (2 inch) piece fresh ginger (20g), grated
2 cloves garlic, crushed
2 small fresh red thai (serrano) chillies,
  chopped finely
⅔ cup (160ml) coconut milk
125g (4 ounces) snow peas, sliced thinly
½ cup finely chopped fresh coriander (cilantro)
75g (2½ ounces) baby asian greens
WONTON CRISPS
12 (100g) wonton wrappers
1 egg white, beaten lightly
2 teaspoons sesame seeds

1 Make wonton crisps.
2 Meanwhile, heat oil in wok; stir-fry chicken until cooked through. Add palm sugar, ginger, garlic and chilli; stir-fry until fragrant. Add coconut milk; cook, uncovered, about 5 minutes or until coconut milk coats chicken mixture, season to taste. Remove from heat; cool 10 minutes.

3 Boil, steam or microwave snow peas until tender, drain; rinse under cold water, drain. Add snow peas to chicken mixture with coriander and salad mix. Toss gently to combine.
4 To serve, layer chicken mixture and wonton crisps on plates.

wonton crisps Preheat oven to 200°C/400°F. Line two oven trays with baking (parchment) paper. Brush wonton wrappers with egg white, fold in half diagonally; brush top with egg white, sprinkle with seeds. Place on trays. Bake about 15 minutes or until crisp.

prep + cook time 35 minutes **serves** 4
nutritional count per serving 22.6g total fat (10.9g saturated fat); 1705kJ (408 cal); 19.5g carbohydrate; 30.2g protein; 3.2g fibre

Baby asian greens, also sold as baby asian salad mix, is a packaged mix of baby buk choy, choy sum, gai lan and water spinach. Available from Asian food stores and most supermarkets.

chilli con carne

1 tablespoon olive oil
500g (1 pound) minced (ground) chicken
1 medium red onion (170g), chopped finely
2 cloves garlic, crushed
2 rindless bacon slices (140g), chopped finely
1 medium red capsicum (bell pepper) (200g),
  chopped finely
1 tablespoon mexican chilli powder
1 fresh long red chilli, chopped finely
800g (28 ounces) canned diced tomatoes
400g (13 ounces) canned kidney beans,
  rinsed, drained
½ cup coarsely chopped fresh coriander (cilantro)

1 Heat half the oil in large saucepan, add chicken, onion, garlic, bacon and capsicum; cook, stirring, until cooked through. Add chilli powder and chilli; cook, stirring, until fragrant.
2 Add undrained tomatoes to pan; simmer, covered, 30 minutes. Add beans; simmer, uncovered, about 15 minutes or until thickened, season to taste. Sprinkle coriander over chilli to serve.
prep + cook time 1 hour **serves** 4
nutritional count per serving 20.3g total fat
(5.4g saturated fat); 1810kJ (433 cal);
20.2g carbohydrate; 38.3g protein; 8.4g fibre
Serve with warmed tortillas and a dollop
of sour cream.

chicken pie with parsnip mash

2 teaspoons vegetable oil
1 medium brown onion (150g), chopped finely
750g (1½ pounds) minced (ground) chicken
1 medium carrot (120g), chopped finely
2 stalks celery (300g), trimmed, chopped finely
¼ cup (35g) plain (all-purpose) flour
1 cup (250ml) chicken stock
2 tablespoons worcestershire sauce
155g (5 ounces) button mushrooms, quartered
¾ cup (120g) frozen peas
PARSNIP MASH
4 medium potatoes (800g), chopped coarsely
2 medium parsnips (500g), chopped coarsely
¼ cup (60ml) milk
45g (1½ ounces) butter
½ cup (40g) finely grated parmesan cheese

1 Make parsnip mash.
2 Preheat oven to 200°C/400°F.
3 Meanwhile, heat oil in large saucepan, add onion and chicken; cook, stirring, until browned. Add carrot and celery; cook, stirring, until soft. Stir in flour then gradually add stock, sauce and mushrooms; cook, stirring, until mixture boils and thickens. Stir in peas; season to taste.
4 Spoon mixture into 2.5-litre (10-cup) ovenproof dish; top with parsnip mash. Bake, uncovered, in oven, about 30 minutes or until browned and heated through.
parsnip mash Boil, steam or microwave potatoes and parsnip until tender; drain. Combine potatoes and parsnip with milk and butter in bowl, mash until smooth; stir in cheese, season to taste.

prep + cook time 1 hour 10 minutes **serves** 6
nutritional count per serving 31.7g total fat (13.5g saturated fat); 2976kJ (712 cal); 49g carbohydrate; 52.4g protein; 10.6g fibre

This pie is suitable to freeze. Thaw in the fridge overnight before reheating.

turkey, pesto and ricotta lasagne

1 tablespoon olive oil
1 medium brown onion (150g), chopped finely
2 cloves garlic, crushed
750g (1½ pounds) minced (ground) turkey
3 cups (750ml) bottled tomato pasta sauce
1 teaspoon dried oregano leaves
2 cups (480g) ricotta cheese
½ cup (40g) finely grated parmesan cheese
½ x 375g packet fresh lasagne
1½ cups (150g) coarsely grated mozzarella cheese
190g (6 ounces) bottled sun-dried tomato pesto

1 Preheat oven to 200°C/400°F.
2 Heat oil in large saucepan, add onion, garlic and turkey; cook, stirring, until browned. Stir in sauce and oregano; simmer, uncovered, about 10 minutes or until thickened, season to taste.
3 Combine ricotta and parmesan in small bowl.

4 Spread ½ cup turkey sauce over base of ovenproof dish (2-litre/8-cup). Top with one lasagne sheet, trimmed to fit. Top with one-third turkey mixture. Spread with one-third of the mozzarella. Repeat layering, finishing with lasagne; spread with pesto then ricotta mixture.
5 Bake, in oven, about 45 minutes or until pasta is tender. Stand 10 minutes before serving.
prep + cook time 1 hour 20 minutes **serves** 6
nutritional count per serving 38.5g total fat
(15.3g saturated fat); 2997kJ (717 cal);
38.9g carbohydrate; 51.5g protein; 5g fibre

We used a thin tomato pasta sauce, also known as sugo or passata, which contains only tomatoes and onion.

sausages with caramelised onion and mustard gravy

Heat 1 tablespoon olive oil in large frying pan; cook 2 thinly sliced medium brown onions (150g) and 2 teaspoons fresh thyme leaves, stirring, about 10 minutes or until caramelised. Stir in 1½ tablespoons plain (all-purpose) flour, then gradually stir in 1 cup chicken stock, ½ cup water and 2 teaspoons dijon mustard. Cook, stirring, until gravy boils and thickens. Heat 2 teaspoons olive oil in medium frying pan; cook 8 thin chicken sausages (560g) until cooked through. Serve sausages with onion and mustard gravy and mashed potatoes.

prep + cook time 25 minutes **serves** 4

nutritional count per serving 38.9g total fat (11.7g saturated fat); 1969kJ (471 cal); 10.6g carbohydrate; 18.5g protein; 4.8g fibre

chicken sausage rolls with barbecue sauce

Preheat oven to 200°C/400°F. Line oven tray with baking paper. Cut 2 ready-rolled puff pastry sheets into 4 squares. Top pastry squares with 8 thin chicken sausages (560g); roll pastry to enclose sausage. Place, seam-side-down, on tray. Bake about 25 minutes or until sausages are cooked through. Combine ½ cup tomato sauce (ketchup), ¼ cup maple syrup, ¼ cup worcestershire sauce and 2 teaspoons dijon mustard in small saucepan. Bring to the boil, simmer, uncovered, about 10 minutes or until thickened slightly; cool 5 minutes. Serve rolls with sauce and a salad.

prep + cook time 30 minutes **makes** 8

nutritional count per roll 25.4g total fat (6g saturated fat); 1630kJ (390 cal); 28.7g carbohydrate; 10.8g protein; 2.8g fibre

chicken and fennel baked risotto

Preheat oven to 200°C/400°F. Heat 1 tablespoon olive oil in flameproof baking dish; cook 6 thin chicken sausages (420g) until cooked through. Remove from pan, slice thinly. Cook 1 finely chopped medium brown onion (150g) and 1 thinly sliced small fennel bulb in same pan until tender. Stir in 1½ cups arborio rice. Add 3 cups chicken stock to pan; bring to the boil. Remove from heat; cover dish with foil. Bake, in oven, 20 minutes, stirring halfway through cooking. Stir in sausages and ⅓ cup chopped fresh flat-leaf parsley leaves. Season to taste.

prep + cook time 45 minutes **serves** 4

nutritional count per serving 29.5g total fat (9.1g saturated fat); 2613kJ (625 cal); 67.2g carbohydrate; 20.3g protein; 4.9g fibre

pesto chicken pizza

Preheat oven to 240°C/475°F. Heat 2 teaspoons olive oil in small frying pan; cook 2 thin chicken sausages (140g) until cooked through. Remove from pan; cut each into 8 thin slices. Line 2 oven trays with baking paper. Place four x 12cm (5 inch) pizza bases on trays. Divide ⅓ cup bottled tomato pasta sauce over bases. Top with ⅓ cup pizza cheese, 4 thinly sliced cherry tomatoes (40g) and sausage slices. Combine 2 tablespoons basil pesto with 2 teaspoons water in small bowl. Drizzle pesto mixture over pizzas. Sprinkle with ⅓ cup pizza cheese. Bake about 12 minutes or until bases are crisp and cheese is browned.

prep + cook time 35 minutes **serves** 4

nutritional count per serving 22.5g total fat (6.9g saturated fat); 2324kJ (556 cal); 64.4g carbohydrate; 20.8g protein; 6g fibre
Pizza bases are available from most supermarkets.

chicken and tomato pasta bake

Preheat oven to 220°C/425°F. Cook 375g (12 ounces) penne pasta in large saucepan of boiling water until tender; drain. Cut one end from 8 thin chicken sausages (560g). Heat 1 tablespoon olive oil in large deep frying pan. Squeeze meat into pan making small meatballs. Add 1 finely chopped medium brown onion (150g); cook, stirring, until meatballs are browned. Stir in undrained 800g (1¾ pounds) canned diced tomatoes; simmer, uncovered, 10 minutes. Stir in ⅔ cup coarsely chopped fresh basil leaves and pasta, season to taste. Spoon into 2.5-litre (10-cup) ovenproof dish. Sprinkle with ¾ cup pizza cheese. Bake about 30 minutes or until browned. Serve with a rocket salad.

prep + cook time 1 hour **serves** 4

nutritional count per serving 41.8g total fat (14.1g saturated fat); 3428kJ (833 cal); 75.2g carbohydrate; 34.4g protein; 9.7g fibre

big breakfast

Preheat oven to 120°C/250°F. Line oven tray with baking paper. Coarsely grate 1 large potato (300g) into small bowl. Divide mixture into 8 portions. Heat 2 teaspoons olive oil in large frying pan; add 4 portions of potato to pan, flattening with spatula. Cook about 4 minutes each side or until golden and tender. Transfer to tray; repeat with remaining potato. Add 8 chicken chipolata sausages (240g), 8 shortcut bacon slices (180g) and 155g (5 ounces) quartered button mushrooms to pan; cook about 7 minutes or until cooked. Transfer to tray; place in oven to keep warm. Crack 4 eggs into pan; cook as you like. Serve eggs with potato, sausages, bacon, mushrooms and ½ cup tomato chutney.

prep + cook time 35 minutes **serves** 4

nutritional count per serving 27.3g total fat (8.7g saturated fat); 1697kJ (406 cal); 13.4g carbohydrate; 25.4g protein; 3.8g fibre

beef & sausage

sticky beef with broccolini and peanuts

1 tablespoon peanut oil
2 cloves garlic, crushed
2.5cm (1 inch) piece fresh ginger (15g), grated
315g (10 ounces) minced (ground) beef
¼ cup (60ml) chinese cooking wine
2 tablespoons char siu sauce
1 tablespoon brown sugar
500g (1 pound) broccolini, trimmed
⅓ cup (45g) coarsely chopped roasted peanuts
1 fresh long red chilli, sliced thinly

1 Heat oil in wok; stir-fry garlic, ginger and beef until beef is browned. Remove beef mixture from wok.
2 Add cooking wine, sauce and sugar to wok; bring to the boil. Reduce heat; simmer, uncovered, 1 minute. Return beef mixture to wok; stir-fry, uncovered, about 2 minutes or until beef mixture is sticky.
3 Meanwhile, boil, steam or microwave broccolini until tender; drain.
4 Serve broccolini topped with beef mixture; sprinkle with nuts and chilli.
prep + cook time 20 minutes **serves** 4
nutritional count per serving 18.1g total fat (4.9g saturated fat); 1329kJ (318 cal); 9.7g carbohydrate; 23.6g protein; 7.5g fibre

spaghetti bolognese

1 tablespoon olive oil
1 medium brown onion (150g), chopped finely
2 cloves garlic, crushed
1 medium carrot (120g), chopped finely
1 stalk celery (150g), trimmed, chopped finely
500g (1 pound) minced (ground) beef
½ cup (125ml) dry red wine
1 cup (250ml) beef stock
⅓ cup (95g) tomato paste
400g (13 ounces) canned crushed tomatoes
1 tablespoon finely chopped fresh oregano
2 tablespoons finely chopped fresh flat-leaf parsley
375g (12 ounces) spaghetti
⅓ cup (25g) flaked parmesan cheese

1 Heat oil in large frying pan, add onion, garlic, carrot and celery; cook, stirring, until vegetables soften. Add beef; stir until browned. Stir in wine, stock, paste, undrained tomatoes and oregano; bring to the boil. Reduce heat; simmer, covered, 30 minutes.
2 Uncover; simmer, a further 30 minutes or until sauce thickens. Remove from heat; stir in parsley, season to taste.
3 Meanwhile, cook spaghetti in large saucepan of boiling water until tender; drain.
4 Serve spaghetti topped with bolognese mixture; sprinkle with cheese.
prep + cook time 1 hour 30 minutes **serves** 4
nutritional count per serving 19.6g total fat (7.2g saturated fat); 2788kJ (667 cal); 73.7g carbohydrate; 39.4g protein; 7.3g fibre

chilli con carne

1 tablespoon olive oil
1 medium brown onion (150g), chopped finely
1 clove garlic, crushed
500g (1 pound) minced (ground) beef
1 teaspoon each ground cumin, coriander and
   dried chilli flakes
1 cup (250ml) beef stock
¼ cup (70g) tomato paste
800g (28 ounces) canned crushed tomatoes
1 tablespoon finely chopped fresh oregano
400g (13 ounces) canned kidney beans,
   rinsed, drained
⅓ cup loosely packed fresh coriander
   (cilantro) leaves
4 flour tortillas, warmed
GUACAMOLE
1 medium avocado (250g)
1 small tomato (90g), seeded, chopped finely
½ small red onion (50g), chopped finely
1 tablespoon lime juice

1 Heat oil in large saucepan, add onion and garlic;
cook, stirring, until onion softens. Add beef and
spices; stir until browned. Stir in stock, paste,
undrained tomatoes and oregano; bring to the
boil. Reduce heat; simmer, covered, 30 minutes.
2 Stir in beans; simmer, uncovered, a further
30 minutes or until thickened slightly, season
to taste.
3 Meanwhile, make guacamole.
4 Serve chilli con carne topped with guacamole;
sprinkle with coriander. Serve with tortillas.
guacamole Mash avocado in medium bowl with
fork until smooth; stir in remaining ingredients,
season to taste.
prep + cook time 1 hour 15 minutes **serves** 4
nutritional count per serving 28.4g total fat
(8.1g saturated fat); 2232kJ (354 cal);
31.2g carbohydrate; 33.9g protein; 9.8g fibre
Serve with steamed rice and sour cream.

beef, spinach and mushroom lasagne

1 tablespoon olive oil
1 medium brown onion (150g), chopped finely
625g (1¼ pounds) minced (ground) beef
½ cup (125ml) dry red wine
2 cups (500ml) beef stock
⅓ cup (95g) tomato paste
400g (13 ounces) canned crushed tomatoes
1 tablespoon finely chopped fresh oregano
30g (1 ounce) butter
315g (10 ounces) swiss brown mushrooms,
   sliced thinly
2 cloves garlic, crushed
625g (1¼ pounds) spinach, trimmed
4 fresh lasagne pasta sheets
⅓ cup (25g) coarsely grated parmesan cheese
WHITE SAUCE
45g (1½ ounces) butter
¼ cup (35g) plain (all-purpose) flour
2 cups (500ml) milk
1 cup (120g) coarsely grated cheddar cheese

1 Preheat oven to 200°C/400°F.
2 Heat oil in large saucepan, add onion: cook, stirring, until soft. Add beef; stir until browned. Stir in wine, stock, paste, undrained tomatoes and oregano; bring to the boil. Reduce heat; simmer, covered, 30 minutes.
3 Uncover; simmer a further 30 minutes or until sauce thickens slightly, season to taste.
4 Make white sauce.
5 Meanwhile, melt butter in large frying pan, add mushrooms and garlic; cook, stirring, until mushrooms soften.
6 Boil, steam or microwave spinach until tender; drain. Squeeze excess liquid from spinach; chop spinach coarsely.
7 Oil shallow ovenproof dish (2.5-litre/10-cup). Cover base with lasagne sheets, cut to fit; top with a third of the beef mixture, a third of the mushrooms and half the white sauce. Top with lasagne sheets, cut to fit; top with another third of the beef mixture, another third of the mushrooms and spinach. Top with remaining trimmed lasagne sheets, remaining beef mixture, remaining mushrooms and remaining white sauce. Sprinkle with cheese.
8 Bake, covered, in oven, about 40 minutes or until pasta is tender.
9 Preheat grill (broiler). Uncover lasagne; grill until browned lightly. Stand 5 minutes before serving.
white sauce Melt butter in medium saucepan; stir in flour until mixture bubbles and thickens. Gradually add milk, stirring, until mixture boils and thickens. Remove from heat; stir in cheese.
prep + cook time 2 hours **serves** 8
nutritional count per serving 26.5g total fat (14.1g saturated fat); 1806kJ (432 cal); 15.9g carbohydrate; 28.1g protein; 5g fibre

sloppy joe jacket potatoes

4 medium potatoes (800g), unpeeled
1 tablespoon olive oil
1 medium brown onion (150g), chopped finely
1 clove garlic, crushed
1 small carrot (70g), chopped finely
1 small red capsicum (bell pepper) (150g),
  chopped finely
1 stalk celery (150g), trimmed, chopped finely
500g (1 pound) minced (ground) beef
1 tablespoon mild american mustard
½ cup (125ml) tomato sauce (ketchup)
⅓ cup (80ml) beef stock
1 tablespoon finely chopped fresh flat-leaf parsley

1 Preheat oven to 220°C/425°F.
2 Wrap potatoes in foil; place in small shallow baking dish. Bake about 1 hour or until tender.
3 Meanwhile, heat oil in large frying pan, add onion, garlic, carrot, capsicum and celery; cook, stirring, until vegetables soften. Add beef; stir until browned. Add mustard, sauce and stock; stir about 5 minutes or until sauce thickens, season to taste.
4 Unwrap potatoes; cut into quarters, without cutting all the way through.
5 Serve potatoes topped with beef mixture; sprinkle with parsley.

prep + cook time 1 hour 10 minutes **serves** 4
nutritional count per serving 16.6g total fat
(5.7g saturated fat); 1835kJ (439 cal);
38.8g carbohydrate; 30.1g protein; 6.6g fibre

sumac beef and pine nut tarts

1 tablespoon olive oil
1 medium brown onion (150g), chopped finely
1 clove garlic, crushed
375g (12 ounces) minced (ground) beef
1 tablespoon sumac
2 teaspoons finely grated lemon rind
2 tablespoons pine nuts
2 sheets ready-rolled puff pastry
1 egg, beaten lightly
125g (4 ounces) grape tomatoes, quartered
¼ cup each coarsely chopped fresh flat-leaf
  parsley and mint
¼ cup (70g) yogurt
2 tablespoons lemon juice

Sumac is a purple-red, astringent spice ground from berries growing on shrubs around the Mediterranean; it has a tart, lemony flavour. It can be found in Middle-Eastern food stores and major supermarkets.

1 Preheat oven to 200°C/400°F. Oil two oven trays.
2 Heat oil in large frying pan, add onion and garlic; cook, stirring, until onion softens. Add beef and sumac; stir until browned. Remove from heat; stir in rind and nuts, season to taste.
3 Cut pastry sheets in half; place on trays. Spoon beef mixture into centre of pastry, brush edges with a little egg; fold edges over to make 2cm (¾ inch) border, press firmly. Brush pastry with remaining egg.
4 Bake tarts about 25 minutes or until browned lightly.
5 Meanwhile, combine tomato and herbs in small bowl; season to taste. Combine yogurt and juice in another small bowl.
6 Serve tarts drizzled with yogurt mixture; top with tomato mixture.

prep + cook time 50 minutes **makes** 4
nutritional count per tart 39.3g total fat (6.9g saturated fat); 2508kJ (600 cal); 34.4g carbohydrate; 26.4g protein; 3.1g fibre

glazed meatloaf

10 slices prosciutto (150g)
500g (1 pound) minced (ground) beef
315g (10 ounces) sausage mince
1 medium carrot (120g), grated coarsely
1 medium zucchini (120g), grated coarsely
1 medium brown onion (150g), chopped finely
1 clove garlic, crushed
1 egg
½ cup (50g) packaged breadcrumbs
⅓ cup (95g) tomato sauce (ketchup)
⅓ cup (95g) barbecue sauce
2 tablespoons light brown sugar
1 tablespoon wholegrain mustard
¼ cup (60ml) water
POTATO MASH
750g (1½ pounds) potatoes, chopped coarsely
30g (1 ounce) butter
½ cup (125ml) hot cream

1 Preheat oven to 200°C/400°F. Oil 15cm x 20cm (6 inch x 8 inch) loaf pan.
2 Line base and sides of pan with prosciutto, leaving overhang on long sides of pan to cover top of loaf.
3 Combine both minces, carrot, zucchini, onion, garlic, egg and breadcrumbs in large bowl; season. Press beef mixture into pan; fold prosciutto over top to cover mixture. Bake, covered, 50 minutes.
4 Meanwhile, combine sauces, sugar and mustard in small bowl.
5 Remove meatloaf from oven; drain juices from pan. Carefully invert meatloaf onto foil-lined oven tray. Brush meatloaf with half the sauce mixture; bake, uncovered, basting occasionally with sauce mixture, about 20 minutes. Stand 10 minutes; slice thickly.
6 Meanwhile, make potato mash.
7 Combine the water with remaining sauce mixture in small saucepan; stir over heat until sugar dissolves. Bring to the boil; simmer, uncovered, about 2 minutes or until sauce thickens slightly.
8 Serve meatloaf with potato mash and sauce.
potato mash Boil, steam or microwave potato until tender; drain. Mash potato in large bowl with butter and cream until smooth, season to taste.

prep + cook time 1 hour 25 minutes **serves** 6
nutritional count per serving 36.1g total fat (18.3g saturated fat); 2575kJ (616 cal); 38.6g carbohydrate; 32.4g protein; 4.7g fibre

If you can't find sausage mince, buy the same weight in sausages and simply squeeze the mince from the sausage skins.

thai beef noodle salad

1 tablespoon peanut oil
500g (1 pound) minced (ground) beef
1 clove garlic, crushed
2.5cm (1 inch) piece fresh ginger (15g), grated
1 fresh long red chilli, chopped finely
185g (6 ounces) rice vermicelli
1 lebanese cucumber (130g), seeded, sliced thinly
250g (8 ounces) cherry tomatoes, halved
1 small red onion (100g), sliced thinly
1 cup each loosely packed fresh mint leaves and
  coriander (cilantro) leaves
¼ cup (60ml) lime juice
2 tablespoons light soy sauce
1 tablespoon fish sauce

1 Heat oil in large frying pan; stir beef, garlic, ginger
and chilli until browned.
2 Meanwhile, place vermicelli in large heatproof
bowl, cover with boiling water; stand until tender,
drain. Rinse under cold water; drain. Using scissors,
cut vermicelli into random lengths.
3 Combine beef mixture and vermicelli in large bowl
with remaining ingredients, season to taste.
prep + cook time 20 minutes **serves** 4
nutritional count per serving 16.4g total fat
(5.9g saturated fat); 1359kJ (325 cal);
16.5g carbohydrate; 25.8g protein; 4.3g fibre

massaman curry

1 fresh long red chilli, chopped coarsely

2 cloves garlic, quartered

10cm (4 inch) stick fresh lemon grass (20g),
  sliced thinly

1 fresh kaffir lime leaf, sliced thinly

2.5cm (1 inch) piece fresh ginger (10g), sliced thinly

1 teaspoon each ground cumin and cinnamon

½ teaspoon each ground coriander, cloves
  and cardamom

2 tablespoons peanut oil

500g (1 pound) minced (ground) beef

1 egg

½ cup (50g) packaged breadcrumbs

625g (1¼ pounds) potatoes, chopped coarsely

3⅓ cups (800ml) light coconut cream

2 tablespoons fish sauce

1 tablespoon tamarind concentrate

1 tablespoon grated palm sugar

⅓ cup (45g) coarsely chopped roasted peanuts

⅓ cup loosely packed fresh coriander
  (cilantro) leaves

1 Blend or process half the chilli, garlic, lemon grass, lime leaf, ginger and spices until finely chopped. With motor operating, gradually add oil in a thin, steady stream until curry paste is smooth.

2 Combine beef, egg and breadcrumbs in medium bowl; roll level tablespoons of mixture into balls. Cook in heated oiled large saucepan until browned; remove from pan.

3 Stir curry paste in heated pan until fragrant. Return meatballs to pan with potato, coconut cream, sauce, tamarind and sugar; bring to the boil. Reduce heat; simmer, uncovered, about 30 minutes or until potato and meatballs are tender, season to taste.

4 Serve curry sprinkled with nuts, coriander and remaining chilli.

prep + cook time 1 hour 10 minutes **serves** 4
nutritional count per serving 60.2g total fat
(36.3g saturated fat); 3503kJ (838 cal);
35.5g carbohydrate; 36.4g protein; 6.9g fibre
Serve with steamed jasmine rice.
To save time, omit step 1 and use bottled massaman curry paste, available from supermarkets.

sweet aussie beef curry

2 teaspoons olive oil
500g (1 pound) minced (ground) beef
30g (1 ounce) butter
1 medium brown onion (150g), chopped finely
2 cloves garlic, crushed
1 medium carrot (120g), chopped finely
1 stalk celery (150g), trimmed, chopped finely
185g (6 ounces) baby new potatoes,
  chopped finely
1 large apple (200g), grated coarsely
1 tablespoon curry powder
1 tablespoon plain (all-purpose) flour
1½ cups (375ml) beef stock
400g (13 ounces) canned crushed tomatoes
1 tablespoon light brown sugar
½ cup (80g) sultanas (golden raisins)
½ cup (60g) frozen peas
⅓ cup coarsely chopped fresh flat-leaf parsley

1 Heat oil in large saucepan, add beef; cook, stirring, until browned. Remove from pan.
2 Melt butter in same pan, add onion, garlic, carrot, celery, potato and apple; cook, stirring, until soft.
3 Return beef to pan with curry powder and flour; cook, stirring, 2 minutes. Gradually stir in stock. Stir in undrained tomatoes, sugar and sultanas; bring to the boil, stirring. Reduce heat; simmer, uncovered, 10 minutes. Stir in peas; cook until hot, season to taste.
4 Sprinkle curry with parsley to serve.
prep + cook time 40 minutes **serves** 6
nutritional count per serving 20.7g total fat (9.5g saturated fat); 1986kJ (475 cal); 39.4g carbohydrate; 29.1g protein; 6.9g fibre
Serve with steamed rice.

beef nachos

2 teaspoons olive oil
500g (1 pound) minced (ground) beef
½ teaspoon dried chilli flakes
1 teaspoon ground cumin
400g (13 ounces) canned diced tomatoes
½ cup (125ml) beef stock
400g (13 ounces) canned kidney beans,
   rinsed, drained
1 medium avocado (250g), chopped coarsely
1 tablespoon lime juice
200g (6½ ounces) corn (tortilla) chips
1 cup (120g) coarsely grated cheddar cheese
½ cup (120g) sour cream
1 medium tomato (150g), chopped finely
2 tablespoons fresh coriander (cilantro) leaves,
   sliced finely

1 Heat oil in large saucepan, add beef, chilli and cumin; cook, stirring, until browned. Stir in undrained tomatoes, stock and beans; bring to the boil. Reduce heat; simmer, uncovered, about 30 minutes or until thickened, season to taste.
2 Meanwhile, mash avocado in small bowl with juice until smooth; season to taste.
3 Preheat grill (broiler).
4 Divide corn chips between four heatproof serving plates; sprinkle with cheese. Grill, in batches, until cheese melts. Top with beef mixture, avocado mixture, sour cream, tomato and coriander.

prep + cook time 45 minutes **serves** 4
nutritional count per serving 59.8g total fat
(27.1g saturated fat); 3699kJ (885 cal);
40.2g carbohydrate; 42g protein; 11.8g fibre

vol au vents

3 sheets ready-rolled puff pastry
1 egg, beaten lightly
1 tablespoon olive oil
500g (1 pound) minced (ground) beef
1 tablespoon plain (all-purpose) flour
2 tablespoons brandy
2 tablespoons worcestershire sauce
½ cup (125ml) beef stock
⅓ cup (80ml) pouring cream
2 tablespoons finely chopped fresh flat-leaf parsley

1 Preheat oven to 220°C/425°F. Oil oven trays.
2 Cut 12 x 12cm (5 inch) rounds from pastry; cut 10cm (4 inch) rounds from centre of eight of the rounds, discard smaller rounds. Place full rounds on trays; brush edges with a little egg. Top each round with one pastry ring; brush with a little more egg. Top with remaining pastry rings; brush with a little more egg. Prick bases with fork; bake about 15 minutes or until browned. Press centres flat with the back of a spoon.
3 Meanwhile, heat oil in large frying pan, add beef; cook, stirring, until browned. Add flour; cook, stirring, 2 minutes. Stir in brandy, sauce, stock and cream; bring to the boil, stirring. Simmer, uncovered, about 10 minutes or until thickened. Remove from heat; stir in half the parsley, season to taste.
4 Divide beef mixture between pastry cases; serve sprinkled with remaining parsley.
prep + cook time 35 minutes **makes** 4
nutritional count per vol au vent 54.6g total fat (13.8g saturated fat); 3524kJ (843 cal); 49.9g carbohydrate; 33.1g protein; 2g fibre

beef, white bean and zucchini pizza

2 teaspoons olive oil
375g (12 ounces) minced (ground) beef
1 medium zucchini (120g)
400g (13 ounces) canned white beans,
 rinsed, drained
1 clove garlic, quartered
1 tablespoon lemon juice
2 large (30cm/12 inch) pizza bases (350g)
⅔ cup (70g) pizza cheese
½ cup (140g) yogurt
1 tablespoon finely chopped fresh mint

1 Preheat oven to 220°C/425°F. Oil oven trays.
2 Heat oil in medium frying pan, add beef; cook, stirring, until browned.
3 Meanwhile, using vegetable peeler, cut zucchini lengthways into thin strips.
4 Blend or process beans, garlic and juice until smooth; season to taste. Spread bean puree over pizza bases. Place bases on trays; top with beef, zucchini and cheese.
5 Bake pizzas about 20 minutes or until bases are crisp. Serve pizzas drizzled with combined yogurt and mint.

prep + cook time 35 minutes **serves** 6
nutritional count per serving 13.2g total fat
(5.2g saturated fat); 1576kJ (377 cal);
37.2g carbohydrate; 24.3g protein; 5.5g fibre

cannelloni with chilli, tomato and basil

2 teaspoons olive oil
1 fresh long red chilli, chopped finely
1kg (2 pounds) tomatoes, chopped coarsely
½ cup firmly packed fresh basil leaves
155g (5 ounces) minced (ground) beef
155g (5 ounces) sausage mince
1 small brown onion (80g), chopped finely
2 cloves garlic, crushed
½ cup (35g) stale breadcrumbs
⅓ cup (80ml) iced water
12 cannelloni tubes (125g)
½ cup (60g) coarsely grated cheddar cheese

1 Preheat oven to 220°C/425°F. Oil large shallow 2.5-litre (10-cup) ovenproof dish.
2 Heat oil in medium saucepan; stir chilli, until fragrant. Add tomato and basil; stir until tomato begin to soften. Bring to the boil; reduce heat. Simmer sauce, uncovered, 30 minutes.

3 Meanwhile, combine minces, onion, garlic, breadcrumbs and the water in medium bowl. Fill cannelloni tubes with mince mixture.
4 Spread half the tomato sauce over base of dish; top with cannelloni tubes, in single layer. Pour remaining sauce over cannelloni; sprinkle with cheese.
5 Bake, covered, 40 minutes. Uncover, bake a further 15 minutes or until browned lightly.

prep + cook time 1 hour 30 minutes **serves** 4
nutritional count per serving 21g total fat (9.2g saturated fat); 1802kJ (431 cal); 34.5g carbohydrate; 23.2g protein; 5.8g fibre

A piping (pastry) bag filled with the chicken mixture will make filling the cannelloni tubes really easy.
If you can't find sausage mince, buy the same weight in sausages and simply squeeze the mince from the sausage skins.

beef dumpling soup

1.5 litres (6 cups) water
2 cups (500ml) beef stock
10cm (4 inch) stick fresh lemon grass (20g),
  halved lengthways
2 fresh kaffir lime leaves
1 tablespoon light soy sauce
1 tablespoon lime juice
500g (1 pound) baby buk choy, chopped coarsely
1 cup (80g) bean sprouts
¼ cup loosely packed fresh coriander
  (cilantro) leaves
1 fresh small red thai (serrano) chilli, sliced finely
BEEF DUMPLINGS
185g (6 ounces) minced (ground) beef
2.5cm (1 inch) piece fresh ginger (10g), grated
1 clove garlic, crushed
1 tablespoon finely chopped fresh coriander (cilantro)
1 tablespoon light soy sauce
1 fresh small thai red (serrano) chilli, chopped finely
20 gow gee wrappers

1 Make beef dumplings.
2 Combine the water, stock, lemon grass and lime leaves in large saucepan; bring to the boil. Reduce heat; simmer broth, uncovered, 15 minutes. Discard lemon grass and lime leaves.
3 Return broth to the boil; add dumplings. Simmer, uncovered, about 5 minutes or until dumplings are cooked through. Stir in sauce and juice.
4 Divide buk choy between serving bowls; ladle over hot broth and dumplings. Serve topped with bean sprouts, coriander and chilli.
beef dumplings Combine mince, ginger, garlic, coriander, sauce and chilli in medium bowl. Place rounded teaspoons of mince mixture in centre of each gow gee wrapper. Brush edges with water; pinch points of wrappers together to completely enclose filling and seal.
prep + cook time 40 minutes **serves** 4
nutritional count per serving 5.4g total fat (2.1g saturated fat); 1062kJ (254 cal); 31g carbohydrate; 18g protein; 3.7g fibre

beef and mushroom stew

375g (12 ounces) minced (ground) beef
30g (1 ounce) butter
250g (8 ounces) swiss brown mushrooms,
  sliced thickly
2 flat mushrooms (160g), halved, sliced thickly
2 cloves garlic, crushed
½ cup (125ml) dry red wine
400g (13 ounces) canned diced tomatoes
1 cup (250ml) beef stock
¼ cup fresh basil leaves
CREAMY POLENTA
2 cups (500ml) water
1 cup (250ml) milk
¾ cup (125g) polenta
½ cup (125ml) (pouring) cream

1 Heat oiled large frying pan, add beef; cook, stirring until browned. Remove from pan.

2 Melt butter in same pan, add mushrooms and garlic; cook, stirring, until mushrooms soften. Return beef to pan with wine; bring to the boil. Boil, uncovered, until liquid reduces by half. Stir in undrained tomatoes and stock; bring to the boil. Reduce heat; simmer, uncovered, about 40 minutes or until thickened slightly, season to taste.

3 Meanwhile, make creamy polenta.

4 Serve stew with polenta; sprinkle with basil.

creamy polenta Bring the water and milk to the boil in medium saucepan; gradually stir in polenta. Cook, stirring, about 5 minutes or until polenta thickens slightly. Stir in cream; season to taste.

prep + cook time 55 minutes **serves** 4
nutritional count per serving 32.1g total fat (18.5g saturated fat); 2291kJ (548 cal); 29.5g carbohydrate; 28.1g protein; 5.1g fibre

arancini with tomato and balsamic sauce

1½ cups (375ml) chicken stock
½ cup (125ml) water
1 tablespoon olive oil
1 small brown onion (80g), chopped finely
1 clove garlic, crushed
½ cup (100g) arborio rice
¼ cup (20g) finely grated parmesan cheese
¼ cup (25g) coarsely grated mozzarella cheese
155g (5 ounces) minced (ground) beef
1 tablespoon tomato paste
2 tablespoons water
½ cup (50g) packaged breadcrumbs
vegetable oil, for deep-frying
TOMATO AND BALSAMIC SAUCE
2 medium tomatoes (300g), chopped coarsely
1 tablespoon balsamic vinegar
2 teaspoons light brown sugar

1 Bring stock and the water to the boil in small saucepan. Reduce heat; simmer, covered.
2 Heat half of the oil in medium saucepan, add onion and garlic; cook, stirring, until soft. Add rice; stir to coat in onion mixture. Stir in ½ cup simmering stock mixture; stir, over medium heat until liquid is absorbed. Continue adding stock, in ½-cup batches, stirring, until liquid is absorbed after each addition. Total cooking time should be about 20 minutes. Remove from heat; stir in cheeses. Cover; refrigerate 30 minutes.

3 Meanwhile, heat remaining oil in small frying pan, add beef; cook, stirring, until browned. Stir in paste and the water; cook, stirring, about 5 minutes or until mixture thickens, season to taste. Cool.
4 Make tomato and balsamic sauce.
5 To make arancini, shape tablespoons of rice mixture into cup shapes in palm of hand; fill with 1 teaspoon beef mixture. Carefully roll rice into balls to enclose filling. Roll arancini in breadcrumbs.
6 Heat oil in deep medium saucepan; deep-fry arancini, in batches, until browned. Drain on absorbent paper. Serve arancini with tomato and balsamic sauce.
tomato and balsamic sauce Combine ingredients in small saucepan; bring to the boil. Reduce heat; simmer, uncovered, stirring, occasionally, about 10 minutes or until sauce thickens, season to taste.
prep + cook time 1 hour (+ refrigeration) **serves** 4
nutritional count per serving 25.9g total fat (6.1g saturated fat); 1818kJ (435 cal); 33.4g carbohydrate; 16.4g protein; 2.2g fibre

You could use ½ cup leftover bolognese mixture to fill the arancini.

beef, cauliflower and bean curry

1 tablespoon olive oil
500g (1 pound) minced (ground) beef
1 medium brown onion (150g), chopped coarsely
1 clove garlic, crushed
1 fresh long red chilli, chopped finely
1 teaspoon each ground cumin and coriander
½ teaspoon each ground turmeric and fennel
400g (13 ounces) canned crushed tomatoes
2 tablespoons tomato paste
1⅔ cups (400ml) coconut cream
315g (10 ounces) cauliflower, cut into florets
155g (5 ounces) green beans, chopped coarsely
¼ cup coarsely chopped fresh mint

1 Heat half the oil in large saucepan, add beef; cook, stirring, until browned. Remove from pan.
2 Heat remaining oil in same pan, add onion, garlic and chilli; cook, stirring, until onion softens. Stir in spices; cook, 2 minutes. Return beef to pan with undrained tomatoes, paste, coconut cream and cauliflower; bring to the boil. Reduce heat; simmer, uncovered, about 20 minutes or until cauliflower is tender.
3 Add beans; simmer, uncovered, until tender.
4 Serve curry sprinkled with mint.
prep + cook time 45 minutes **serves** 4
nutritional count per serving 37.3g total fat (23.8g saturated fat); 2149kJ (514 cal); 12.9g carbohydrate; 29.5g protein; 6.7g fibre

sweet chilli and plum beef noodles

1 tablespoon peanut oil
375g (12 ounces) minced (ground) beef
1 clove garlic, crushed
1 fresh long red chilli, sliced thinly
2.5cm (1 inch) piece fresh ginger (10g), grated
1 small red onion (80g), sliced thinly
1 small red capsicum (bell pepper) (150g),
  sliced thinly
1 packet hokkien noodles (450g)
¼ cup (60ml) sweet chilli sauce
2 tablespoons plum sauce
2 tablespoons light soy sauce
155g (5 ounces) sugar snap peas, trimmed
⅓ cup firmly packed fresh coriander
  (cilantro) leaves

1 Heat half of the oil in wok; stir-fry beef, garlic, chilli and ginger until beef is browned. Remove from wok.
2 Heat remaining oil in wok; stir-fry onion and capsicum until tender. Return beef mixture to wok with noodles and sauces; stir-fry until heated through. Add peas; stir-fry until hot.
3 Serve stir-fry sprinkled with coriander.
prep + cook time 25 minutes **serves** 4
nutritional count per serving 15.1g total fat
(4.9g saturated fat); 2362kJ (565 cal);
73.1g carbohydrate; 30.8g protein; 4.9g fibre

If you can't buy hokkien noodles, use fresh wide egg noodles.

rigatoni bake with herb crumb

30g (1 ounce) butter
1 medium brown onion (150g), chopped finely
1 clove garlic, crushed
1 medium carrot (120g), chopped finely
500g (1 pound) minced (ground) beef
1 cup (250ml) milk
3 cups (750ml) bottled tomato pasta sauce
375g (12 ounces) rigatoni pasta
⅔ cup (70g) pizza cheese
½ cup (35g) stale breadcrumbs
2 teaspoons finely grated lemon rind
2 tablespoons finely chopped fresh flat-leaf parsley

1 Melt butter in large saucepan, add onion, garlic and carrot; cook, stirring, until onion softens. Add beef; cook, stirring, until browned. Add milk; cook, stirring occasionally, until liquid reduces by half. Add sauce; simmer, uncovered, about 30 minutes or until sauce thickens, season to taste.
2 Meanwhile, cook pasta in large saucepan of boiling water until tender; drain.
3 Preheat oven to 220°C/425°F. Oil ovenproof dish (2.5-litre/10-cup).
4 Stir pasta and cheese into beef mixture; spoon into dish. Sprinkle with combined breadcrumbs, rind and parsley. Bake, uncovered, about 30 minutes or until browned lightly. Stand 10 minutes before serving, topped with extra finely shredded parsley and rind.
prep + cook time 1 hour 20 minutes **serves** 6
nutritional count per serving 18g total fat (9.1g saturated fat); 2353kJ (562 cal); 65.7g carbohydrate; 30.8g protein; 6.2g fibre

stuffed eggplants

2 medium eggplants (600g)
1 tablespoon olive oil
1 small brown onion (80g), chopped finely
1 clove garlic, crushed
315g (10 ounces) minced (ground) beef
2 teaspoons ground allspice
1 medium tomato (150g), chopped finely
1 teaspoon finely grated lemon rind
1 tablespoon lemon juice
2 tablespoons finely chopped fresh flat-leaf parsley
100g soft fetta cheese, crumbled
⅓ cup (25g) stale breadcrumbs

1   Cut tops from eggplants; cook eggplants in medium saucepan of boiling water 6 minutes. Drain; halve lengthways.

2   Using small sharp knife, carefully remove flesh from eggplant halves, leaving a 1cm (½ inch) border; chop flesh finely.
3   Heat oil in large frying pan, add onion and garlic; cook, stirring, until soft. Add beef; cook, stirring, until browned. Add eggplant flesh, allspice and tomato; cook, stirring, until eggplant is tender. Remove from heat; stir in rind, juice and half the parsley, season to taste.
4   Preheat oven to 200°C/400°F. Oil medium shallow baking dish.
5   Place eggplant halves in dish; fill with beef mixture. Sprinkle with combined remaining parsley, cheese and breadcrumbs. Bake uncovered, about 30 minutes or until eggplants are tender.
prep + cook time 1 hour 10 minutes **serves** 4
nutritional count per serving 18.4g total fat (7.7g saturated fat); 1258kJ (301 cal); 9.9g carbohydrate; 22.1g protein; 4.4g fibre

warm beef, orange and date salad

315g (10 ounces) minced (ground) beef
2 teaspoons ground cumin
1 medium orange (240g)
1 small bunch (300g) watercress, trimmed
400g (13 ounces) canned chickpeas (garbanzos),
  rinsed, drained
8 fresh dates, seeded, sliced thinly
2 tablespoons white wine vinegar
1 tablespoon olive oil

1 Heat oiled small frying pan, add beef and cumin; cook, stirring, until browned.
2 Meanwhile, segment orange over small bowl; reserve 2 tablespoons juice.
3 Combine beef mixture, orange segments and reserved juice with remaining ingredients in large bowl, season to taste.

prep + cook time 25 minutes **serves** 4
nutritional count per serving 13.6g total fat
(4g saturated fat); 1413kJ (338 cal);
27.8g carbohydrate; 21.8g protein; 8.9g fibre

sweet and sour sausage kebabs

Cook 6 thin beef sausages (480g) in medium saucepan of boiling water until cooked; drain, cut into 2.5cm (1 inch) pieces. Cut 1 red capsicum (bell pepper) and ½ small pineapple into 2.5cm (1 inch) pieces. Cut 1 red onion into thin wedges. Thread sausages, capsicum, pineapple and onion onto 8 bamboo skewers; brush with ⅓ cup sweet and sour sauce. Cook skewers on heated oiled grill plate (or grill or barbecue) until browned. Serve drizzled with an extra 2 tablespoons sweet and sour sauce; sprinkle with 2 tablespoons coarsely chopped fresh coriander (cilantro).
prep + cook time 25 minutes **makes** 8
nutritional count per skewer 15.8g total fat (7.4g saturated fat); 1083kJ (259 cal); 18.9g carbohydrate; 8.6g protein; 3.7g fibre
Soak bamboo skewers in cold water for at least 30 minutes before using to prevent them from scorching during cooking.

sausages with red cabbage

Cook 6 thick beef sausages (900g) in heated oiled large frying pan until cooked; slice lengthways. Cook 6 cups shredded red cabbage in pan, stirring, about 5 minutes or until softened. Add 2 tablespoons red wine vinegar and 1 tablespoon light brown sugar; cook, stirring, about 10 minutes or until liquid evaporates. Return sausages to pan; cook, stirring, until heated through. Remove from heat; stir in ½ cup chopped fresh flat-leaf parsley, season to taste.
prep + cook time 30 minutes **serves** 4
nutritional count per serving 57.6g total fat (27.5g saturated fat); 2930kJ (701 cal); 12.3g carbohydrate; 29.4g protein; 11.8g fibre

sausage, tomato and basil frittata

Cook 6 beef chipolatas (180g) in heated oiled 23cm-base (9 inch) frying pan until cooked through. Drain on absorbent paper; chop coarsely. Drain excess fat from pan. Return sausages to heated pan with 250g (8 ounces) grape tomatoes. Combine 6 eggs, ½ cup pouring cream, ¼ cup finely shredded fresh basil and ½ cup coarsely grated cheddar cheese in large jug; season. Pour egg mixture over sausages; cook over low heat about 5 minutes or until frittata is almost set. Meanwhile, preheat grill (broiler). Cook frittata under grill about 5 minutes or until set.
prep + cook time 25 minutes **serves** 4
nutritional count per serving 38.8g total fat (20.6g saturated fat); 1860kJ (445 cal); 3.5g carbohydrate; 20.6g protein; 2.2g fibre

black bean sausage stir-fry

Cook 6 thick beef sausages (900g) in medium saucepan of boiling water until cooked through; drain, slice thinly. Stir fry sausages in heated oiled wok until browned. Add 1 thickly sliced medium red capsicum (bell pepper) and 1 thickly sliced medium red onion; stir-fry until vegetables are tender. Add 185g (6 ounces) trimmed snow peas, 1 tablespoon black bean sauce, ¼ cup beef stock and 2 tablespoons water; stir-fry until heated through.

prep + cook time 25 minutes **serves** 4
nutritional count per serving 57.5g total fat (27.5g saturated fat); 2888kJ (691 cal); 11.9g carbohydrate; 29.1g protein; 8.1g fibre

sausage rolls with beetroot relish

Cook 4 thin beef sausages (320g) in heated oiled medium frying pan until cooked through. Meanwhile, combine 1 coarsely grated large uncooked trimmed beetroot, 1 tablespoon red wine vinegar, 1 teaspoon wholegrain mustard and ⅓ cup coarsely chopped fresh flat-leaf parsley in medium bowl; season to taste. Divide sausages and beetroot relish between 4 long bread rolls.

prep + cook time 15 minutes **serves** 4
nutritional count per serving 23.1g total fat (10.1g saturated fat); 1906kJ (456 cal); 42.5g carbohydrate; 16.6g protein; 6.3g fibre

sausages with the lot

Cook 12 beef chipolatas (360g) in heated oiled medium frying pan until cooked through; remove from pan. Cook 1 thickly sliced large brown onion in same heated pan until onion softens. Add 4 coarsely chopped medium tomatoes and ½ teaspoon dried chilli flakes; cook, stirring occasionally, about 10 minutes or until tomato softens, season to taste. Meanwhile, preheat grill (broiler). Return sausages to pan. Carefully crack 4 eggs into pan; cook under grill about 5 minutes or until eggs are just set. Serve sprinkled with ⅓ cup coarsely chopped fresh flat-leaf parsley.

prep + cook time 35 minutes **serves** 4
nutritional count per serving 28.3g total fat (12.6g saturated fat); 1530kJ (366 cal); 6.9g carbohydrate; 19.2g protein; 4.9g fibre

rösti baskets with beef and salsa verde

3 medium potatoes (600g), unpeeled
30g (1 ounce) butter, melted
1 tablespoon olive oil
1 small brown onion (80g), chopped finely
1 clove garlic, crushed
500g (1 pound) minced (ground) beef
1 tablespoon plain (all-purpose) flour
¾ cup (180ml) beef stock
SALSA VERDE
⅓ cup finely chopped fresh flat-leaf parsley
2 tablespoons finely chopped fresh basil
1 tablespoon finely chopped fresh mint
1 clove garlic, crushed
1 teaspoon dijon mustard
1 tablespoon red wine vinegar
2 tablespoons olive oil
1 tablespoon rinsed, drained capers,
  chopped finely

1   Cover whole potatoes with cold water in medium saucepan; bring to the boil. Boil, covered, about 20 minutes or until almost tender; drain. Cool, then peel potatoes; grate coarsely. Combine potato and butter in medium bowl, season to taste.
2   Preheat oven to 220°C/425°F.
3   To make rösti, press potato mixture firmly over bases and sides of six-hole texas muffin pan (¾-cup/180ml). Bake rösti about 45 minutes or until crisp. Stand rösti in pan 5 minutes before turning out onto absorbent paper.
4   Meanwhile, make salsa verde.
5   Heat oil in large frying pan, add onion and garlic; cook, stirring, until soft. Add beef; cook, stirring, until browned. Add flour; stir 2 minutes. Gradually stir in stock until mixture boils and thickens.
6   Divide beef mixture between rösti; top with salsa verde.
salsa verde Combine ingredients in small bowl; season to taste.
prep + cook time 1 hour 20 minutes (+ cooling)
makes 6
nutritional count per serving 21.1g total fat (7.4g saturated fat); 1346kJ (322 cal); 13.8g carbohydrate; 18.4g protein; 2.1g fibre

meat pies

1 tablespoon olive oil
1 medium brown onion (150g), chopped finely
2 rindless bacon slices (130g), chopped finely
500g (1 pound) minced (ground) beef
¼ cup (35g) plain (all-purpose) flour
2 cups (500ml) beef stock
¼ cup (70g) tomato paste
1 tablespoon worcestershire sauce
5 sheets ready-rolled shortcrust pastry
1 egg, beaten lightly

1 Heat oil in large saucepan, add onion and bacon; cook, stirring, until onion softens. Add beef; cook, stirring, until browned. Add flour; cook, stirring, 2 minutes. Gradually stir in stock, paste and sauce; bring to the boil, stirring. Reduce heat; simmer, uncovered, about 10 minutes or until thickened, season to taste. Cool.

2 Preheat oven to 200°C/400°F. Oil six ¾-cup (180ml) pie dishes.

3 Cut six 15cm (6 inch) rounds and six 12cm (5 inch) rounds from pastry; press large rounds into base and sides of pie dishes. Prick bases with fork. Divide beef mixture between pie cases, brush edges with a little egg; top with small pastry rounds, pressing edges together firmly. Brush pies with egg, cut small slits in pastry tops.

4 Bake about 30 minutes or until browned lightly.

prep + cook time 1 hour **makes** 6
nutritional count per pie 52.9g total fat (25.3g saturated fat); 3708kJ (887 cal); 69.6g carbohydrate; 32g protein; 3.6g fibre

old-fashioned rissoles with gravy

1 tablespoon olive oil
1 medium brown onion (150g), chopped finely
1 clove garlic, crushed
2 rindless bacon slices (130g), chopped finely
500g (1 pound) minced (ground) beef
1 egg
½ cup (50g) packaged breadcrumbs
1 small carrot (70g), grated finely
⅓ cup coarsely chopped fresh flat-leaf parsley
1½ tablespoons plain (all-purpose) flour
1½ cups (375ml) beef stock

1 Heat oil in large frying pan, add onion, garlic and bacon; cook, stirring, until onion softens. Remove from pan; cool. Drain excess fat from pan.

2 Combine onion mixture, beef, egg, breadcrumbs, carrot and parsley in medium bowl; shape mixture into eight patties.
3 Cook patties in same heated pan about 15 minutes or until browned and cooked through. Remove from pan; cover to keep warm. Reserve pan with drippings.
4 Cook flour in same pan, stirring, until mixture browns and bubbles. Gradually stir in stock; cook, stirring, until gravy boils and thickens, strain into large heatproof jug. Serve rissoles with gravy.
prep + cook time 40 minutes **serves** 4
nutritional count per serving 22.5g total fat
(7.8g saturated fat); 1701kJ (407 cal);
15.7g carbohydrate; 35.2g protein; 0g fibre
Serve with mashed potato.

sausage rolls

500g (1 pound) minced (ground) beef
500g (1 pound) sausage mince
1 medium brown onion (150g), chopped finely
½ cup (50g) packaged breadcrumbs
1 egg
2 tablespoons finely chopped fresh flat-leaf parsley
2 tablespoons tomato paste
2 tablespoons barbecue sauce
4 sheets ready-rolled puff pastry
1 egg, beaten lightly, extra

1 Preheat oven to 220°C/425°F. Oil and line oven trays with baking (parchment) paper.
2 Combine minces, onion, breadcrumbs, egg, parsley, paste and sauce in large bowl; season.
3 Cut pastry sheets in half lengthways. Spoon or pipe mince mixture lengthways along centre of each pastry piece; roll pastry over to enclose filling. Cut each roll into two pieces; place rolls, seam-side down, on trays. Brush with extra egg; cut slits into tops of rolls. Bake about 30 minutes.

prep + cook time 45 minutes **makes** 16
nutritional count per roll 20.5g total fat
5.4g saturated fat); 1333kJ (319 cal);
20g carbohydrate; 13.3g protein; 1.5g fibre

Use a large piping (pastry) bag without a tube, to pipe the mixture onto the pastry: it's easier than spooning.
For small party sausage rolls, cut each roll into six pieces and bake about 25 minutes.
If you can't find sausage mince, buy the same weight in sausages and simply squeeze the mince from the sausage skins.

meat-lovers' scrolls

2 teaspoons olive oil
1 small brown onion (80g), chopped finely
155g (5 ounces) minced (ground) beef
155g (5 ounces) sausage mince
2 cups (300g) self-raising flour
1 tablespoon caster (superfine) sugar
30g (1 ounce) cold butter, chopped
¾ cup (180ml) milk
⅓ cup (80ml) barbecue sauce
1 cup (110g) pizza cheese
30g (1 ounce) baby spinach leaves
1 egg, beaten lightly

1 Preheat oven to 200°C/400°F. Oil 25cm x 35cm (10 inch x 14 inch) swiss roll pan.
2 Heat oil in small frying pan, add onion; cook, stirring, until soft. Add minces; cook, stirring, until browned, season to taste. Cool.
3 Sift flour and sugar into medium bowl; rub in butter. Stir in milk; mix to a soft, sticky dough. Knead dough on floured surface; roll dough into 30cm x 40cm (12 inch x 16 inch) rectangle.
4 Spread dough with sauce; sprinkle with mince mixture, cheese and spinach. Roll dough tightly from long side; trim ends. Cut roll into 12 slices; place scrolls, cut-side-up, in pan. Brush scrolls with a little egg; bake about 30 minutes or until browned. Serve scrolls warm or cold.
prep + cook time 1 hour **makes** 12
nutritional count per scroll 10.4g total fat (5.2g saturated fat); 986kJ (236 cal); 24.4g carbohydrate; 10.4g protein; 1.5g fibre

If you can't find sausage mince, buy the same weight in sausages and simply squeeze the mince from the sausage skins.

beef bourguignon and potato pie

500g (1 pound) minced (ground) beef
30g (1 ounce) butter
1 medium brown onion (150g), chopped finely
4 rindless bacon slices (260g), chopped finely
155g (5 ounces) button mushrooms, sliced thinly
2 cloves garlic, crushed
2 tablespoons plain (all-purpose) flour
1 cup (250ml) dry red wine
1 cup (250ml) beef stock
2 tablespoons tomato paste
2 fresh bay leaves
1kg (2 pounds) potatoes, chopped coarsely
30g (1 ounce) butter, extra
⅓ cup (80ml) pouring cream, heated

1 Heat oiled large saucepan, add beef; cook, stirring, until browned, then remove from pan.
2 Melt butter in same pan, add onion, bacon, mushrooms and garlic; cook, stirring, until vegetables soften. Return beef to pan with flour; cook, stirring, 2 minutes. Stir in wine, stock, paste and bay leaves; bring to the boil, stirring. Reduce heat; simmer, uncovered, about 45 minutes or until thickened. Discard bay leaves.
3 Meanwhile, boil, steam or microwave potatoes until tender; drain. Push potato through fine sieve into large bowl; stir in butter and cream until smooth.
4 Preheat grill (broiler).
5 Spoon beef mixture into oiled 1.5-litre (6-cup) ovenproof dish; top with potato. Grill about 5 minutes or until browned lightly.
prep + cook time 1 hour 20 minutes **serves** 4
nutritional count per serving 41.7g total fat (22.1g saturated fat); 3148kJ (753 cal); 36.6g carbohydrate; 45.1g protein; 5.8g fibre

nutty beef burgers

Combine 500g (1 pound) minced (ground) beef, 1 egg and ⅓ cup finely chopped roasted unsalted pistachios in medium bowl; shape mixture into four patties. Cook patties in heated oiled medium frying pan until cooked through. Meanwhile, using vegetable peeler, cut 1 lebanese cucumber lengthways into thin strips. Divide cucumber, patties and ½ cup aïoli between four split and toasted turkish bread rolls; season to taste.
prep + cook time 20 minutes **serves** 4
nutritional count per serving 51.1g total fat (10.8g saturated fat); 3979kJ (952 cal); 79.2g carbohydrate; 40.7g protein; 6.8g fibre
Use a whole-egg mayonnaise instead of the aïoli, if you prefer.

napoletana meatball baguette

Combine 500g (1 pound) minced (ground) beef, 1 egg and ½ cup stale breadcrumbs in medium bowl; roll rounded tablespoons of mixture into balls, flatten slightly. Cook meatballs in heated oiled large frying pan until browned. Add 1½ cups bottled tomato pasta sauce; bring to the boil. Reduce heat; simmer, uncovered, about 5 minutes or until meatballs are cooked through, season to taste. Cut 1 sourdough baguette in half horizontally, without cutting all the way through. Fill baguette with meatballs and sauce; sprinkle with 1 cup pizza cheese. Cut bread stick into four.
prep + cook time 30 minutes **serves** 4
nutritional count per serving 24.2g total fat (10g saturated fat); 3035kJ (726 cal); 77g carbohydrate; 45.9g protein; 6.6g fibre

lemon grass beef lettuce wraps

Heat oiled wok; stir-fry 1 finely chopped 10cm (4 inch) stick fresh lemon grass until fragrant. Add 625g (1¼ pounds) minced (ground) beef; stir-fry until browned. Add 2 tablespoons each kecap manis and sweet chilli sauce; stir-fry until hot. Remove from heat; stir in 1 cup coarsely chopped bean sprouts, season to taste. Divide mince mixture between 8 large iceberg lettuce leaves.
prep + cook time 15 minutes **serves** 4
nutritional count per serving 14.7g total fat (6.3g saturated fat); 1120kJ (268 cal); 2.7g carbohydrate; 30.5g protein; 1.6g fibre

beef and white bean pitta pockets

Cook 375g (12 ounces) minced (ground) beef and 2 teaspoons ground cumin in heated oiled large frying pan until browned, season to taste. Meanwhile, blend or process 400g (13 ounces) canned rinsed and drained white beans and 2 tablespoons lemon juice until smooth. With motor operating, gradually add enough water (about ¼ cup) to make puree pourable, season to taste. Divide beef mixture and 2 cups finely shredded butter lettuce between 4 halved and split pitta pockets. Drizzle with white bean puree. Serve with yogurt.

prep + cook time 25 minutes **serves** 4
nutritional count per serving 10g total fat (3.9g saturated fat); 1313kJ (314 cal); 27.3g carbohydrate; 25.4g protein; 5.9g fibre

beef and bean enchiladas

Cook 625g (1¼ pounds) minced (ground) beef in heated oiled large frying pan until browned. Add 400g (13 ounces) rinsed and drained canned kidney beans, 35g (1 ounce) packet taco seasoning mix and ½ cup thick and chunky tomato salsa; cook, stirring, about 2 minutes or until hot, season to taste. Preheat grill (broiler). Divide mince mixture between four 20cm (8 inch) flour tortillas; roll tortillas tightly to enclose filling. Place tortillas in small shallow baking dish; drizzle with a further ½ cup salsa, sprinkle with 1 cup grated cheddar cheese. Grill enchiladas about 5 minutes or until cheese melts.

prep + cook time 25 minutes **serves** 4
nutritional count per serving 28.2g total fat (13.2g saturated fat); 2525kJ (604 cal); 38.2g carbohydrate; 45.8g protein; 6.9g fibre

open caprese burgers

Shape 375g (12 ounces) sausage mince into four thin patties. Cook patties in heated oiled large frying pan until cooked through. Divide patties, 2 thinly sliced medium tomatoes, 4 thinly sliced cherry bocconcini cheese and ⅓ cup loosely packed fresh basil leaves between 4 toasted thick slices ciabatta bread. Drizzle with 1 tablespoon balsamic vinegar; season to taste.

prep + cook time 20 minutes **serves** 4
nutritional count per serving 25.2g total fat (10.9g saturated fat); 1705kJ (408 cal); 26.3g carbohydrate; 17.4g protein; 4.2g fibre

lamb

moussaka

¼ cup (60ml) olive oil
1 medium eggplant (300g), sliced thinly lengthways
1 medium brown onion (150g), chopped finely
2 cloves garlic, chopped finely
750g (1½ pounds) minced (ground) lamb
185g (6 ounces) button mushrooms,
  chopped coarsely
½ cup (125ml) dry white wine
400g (13 ounces) canned crushed tomatoes
1 tablespoon tomato paste
3 teaspoons dried oregano
½ cup coarsely chopped fresh flat-leaf parsley
¼ cup (20g) finely grated parmesan cheese
YOGURT SAUCE
1½ cups (420g) greek-style yogurt
2 eggs, beaten lightly
2 tablespoons (all-purpose) plain flour

1 Heat 1 tablespoon of the oil in large frying pan, cook one-third of the eggplant until browned both sides; drain on absorbent paper. Repeat with remaining oil and eggplant.

2 Reheat same pan, add onion and garlic; cook, stirring, until soft. Add lamb and mushrooms; cook, stirring, until browned. Add wine, undrained tomatoes, tomato paste and oregano; simmer, uncovered, stirring occasionally, about 35 minutes or until liquid is almost evaporated. Remove from heat; stir in parsley, season to taste.

3 Preheat oven to 180°C/350°F.

4 Oil 20cm (8 inch) square ovenproof dish. Slightly overlap one-third of the eggplant in base of dish; spread with one-third of the lamb mixture. Repeat twice with remaining eggplant and lamb mixture.

5 Make yogurt sauce.

6 Spoon yogurt sauce over lamb mixture; sprinkle with cheese. Bake about 30 minutes or until browned lightly and heated through. Serve hot or cold, sprinkled with grated parmesan cheese, if you like.

yogurt sauce Combine ingredients in medium bowl; season.

prep + cook time 1 hour 50 minutes **serves** 6
nutritional count per serving 27.1g total fat (9.8g saturated fat); 1881kJ (450 cal); 11.4g carbohydrate; 35.5g protein; 3.8g fibre
Serve with a green salad.

lamb with snake beans

1½ cups (300g) jasmine rice
1 tablespoon peanut oil
2 shallots (50g), sliced thinly
2 cloves garlic, crushed
3cm (1 inch) piece fresh ginger (15g), grated
1 fresh small red thai (serrano) chilli, sliced thinly
500g (1 pound) minced (ground) lamb
1 cup (250ml) chicken stock
2 tablespoons fish sauce
1½ tablespoons grated palm sugar
2 teaspoons finely grated lime rind
315g (10 ounces) snake beans, chopped coarsely
2 tablespoons lime juice
1 cup loosely packed fresh coriander
  (cilantro) leaves
1 cup loosely packed fresh thai basil leaves

1 Cook rice according to packet directions; cover to keep warm.
2 Meanwhile, heat wok over high heat, add oil; stir-fry shallots, garlic, ginger and chilli until fragrant. Add lamb; stir-fry until browned.
3 Stir in stock, sauce, sugar and rind; bring to the boil. Add beans; stir until tender. Stir in juice and herbs.
4 Serve lamb mixture with rice and lime wedges.

prep + cook time 30 minutes **serves** 4
nutritional count per serving 17.8g total fat (6.8g saturated fat); 2437kJ (583 cal); 67.5g carbohydrate; 35.4g protein; 4.1g fibre

Snake beans are long (about 40cm), thin, round, fresh green beans, Asian in origin, with a taste similar to green or french beans. They are also called yard-long beans because of their (pre-metric) length. If snake beans are unavailable, use green beans.

lamb, potato and rosemary pies

1 tablespoon olive oil
1 medium brown onion (150g), chopped coarsely
2 cloves garlic, chopped finely
1 tablespoon coarsely chopped fresh rosemary
625g (1¼ pounds) minced (ground) lamb
½ cup (125ml) dry white wine
1 cup (250ml) beef or chicken stock
1 tablespoon finely grated lemon rind
2 medium potatoes (400g), chopped coarsely
1 sheet ready-rolled puff pastry
1 egg, beaten lightly
CHUNKY TOMATO SAUCE
5 large ripe egg (plum) tomatoes (450g),
  chopped coarsely
¼ cup (60ml) brown malt vinegar
¼ cup (55g) light brown sugar

1 Heat oil in medium heavy-based saucepan, add onion, garlic and rosemary; cook, stirring, until onion is soft. Add lamb; stir until browned. Add wine, stock and rind; bring to a simmer. Add potato; simmer, uncovered, stirring occasionally, about 35 minutes or until potato is tender, season to taste.

2 Meanwhile, make chunky tomato sauce.

3 Preheat oven to 200°C/400°F.

4 Divide lamb mixture between four 1¼-cup (310ml) ovenproof dishes. Cut four 12cm (5 inch) rounds from pastry; top dishes with pastry, brush with egg. Bake about 20 minutes or until browned. Serve pies with chunky tomato sauce.

chunky tomato sauce Combine ingredients in medium saucepan; bring to the boil. Reduce heat, simmer, uncovered, about 25 minutes or until thickened. Cool.

prep + cook time 1 hour 15 minutes **serves** 4
nutritional count per serving 31.2g total fat
(9.1g saturated fat); 2642kJ (632 cal);
40.5g carbohydrate; 40.5g protein; 4.1g fibre

lamb kofta curry

1 tablespoon vegetable oil
1 medium brown onion (150g), chopped finely
2 cloves garlic, chopped finely
2 tablespoons mild curry powder
400g (13 ounces) canned chopped tomatoes
½ cup (125 ml) chicken stock
1 cup (280g) greek-style yogurt
1½ cups (300g) basmati rice
½ cup loosely packed fresh coriander
   (cilantro) leaves
LAMB KOFTA
1 small brown onion (80g), chopped coarsely
5cm (2 inch) piece fresh ginger (20g),
   chopped coarsely
2 cloves garlic, chopped coarsely
1 fresh small green chilli, chopped coarsely
750g (1½ pounds) minced (ground) lamb
½ cup (140g) greek-style yogurt
1 egg, beaten lightly
1½ teaspoons garam marsala

1 Make lamb kofta.
2 Heat oil in heavy wide-based saucepan over medium heat, add onion, garlic and curry powder; cook, stirring, until onion softens. Stir in tomatoes and stock; bring to the boil. Reduce heat; simmer. Stir in yogurt.
3 Add kofta to simmering sauce, turn to coat in sauce. Simmer, uncovered, about 40 minutes or until kofta are cooked through and sauce is thickened, season to taste.
4 Meanwhile, cook rice according to packet directions.
5 Serve kofta with rice; sprinkle with coriander.
lamb kofta Process onion, ginger, garlic and chilli until finely chopped; transfer to large bowl. Stir in remaining ingredients. Roll mixture into 24 meatballs; place on tray, cover, refrigerate 1 hour.
prep time + cook 1 hour 10 minutes (+ refrigeration)
serves 6
nutritional count per serving 19.2g total fat (8.1g saturated fat); 2123kJ (508 cal); 47.5g carbohydrate; 34.8g protein; 2.4g fibre

Curry can be made up to three days ahead or can be frozen for up to three months in an airtight container.

lamb spanakopita

1 tablespoon olive oil
1 medium brown onion (150g), chopped coarsely
2 cloves garlic, chopped finely
625g (1¼ pounds) minced (ground) lamb
2 teaspoons dried oregano
60g (2 ounces) butter, melted
8 sheets fillo pastry
SILVER BEET AND CHEESE FILLING
½ bunch (500g) silver beet (swiss chard)
1 tablespoon olive oil
1¼ cups (300g) ricotta cheese
185g (6 ounces) fetta cheese, crumbled
2 teaspoons finely grated lemon rind
¼ cup finely shredded fresh mint

1 Heat oil in large frying pan, add onion and garlic; cook, stirring, until soft. Add lamb and oregano; stir until cooked through, season to taste.
2 Make silver beet and cheese filling.
3 Preheat oven to 220°C/425°F.
4 Brush 20cm (8 inch) loose-based square cake pan with a little of the butter. Layer three pastry sheets, brushing each sheet with butter. Place in cake pan to cover base and two opposite sides with edges overhanging. Brush top pastry sheet with butter. Repeat with three more sheets, placing crossways over sheets in pan.
5 Spread half the lamb mixture over pastry base then half the filling; repeat with remaining lamb mixture and filling. Fold overhanging pastry over filling. Layer remaining sheets of pastry, brushing each with butter, fold to fit top of pie. Brush with butter.
6 Bake about 25 minutes or until pastry is browned lightly. Serve hot or at room temperature; accompany with lemon wedges.
silver beet and cheese filling Finely slice silver beet stems and leaves separately. Heat oil in large frying pan, add stems; cook, stirring, until tender. Add leaves; cook, stirring, until soft. Remove from heat; stir in ricotta, fetta, rind and mint, season to taste.
prep + cook time 1 hour 10 minutes **serves** 6
nutritional count per serving 38.1g total fat (19.5g saturated fat); 2324kJ (556 cal); 16.4g carbohydrate; 36.2g protein; 3.3g fibre
Serve with a green salad.

lamb, potato and okra curry

1 medium brown onion (150g), chopped coarsely
½ cup (50g) mild curry paste
750g (1½ pounds) minced (ground) lamb
½ cup (125ml) water
400g (13 ounces) canned tomato puree
2 medium potatoes (400g), chopped coarsely
185g (6 ounces) okra, trimmed

1 Heat large oiled saucepan; stir onion and curry paste, until onion softens. Add lamb; stir until browned.
2 Add the water and puree; bring to the boil. Add potato; simmer, covered, about 25 minutes or until potato is tender. Add okra; simmer, covered, about 15 minutes or until tender. Season to taste.

prep + cook time 50 minutes **serves** 6
nutritional count per serving 15.1g total fat (6g saturated fat); 1321kJ (316 cal); 13.3g carbohydrate; 29.5g protein; 4.5g fibre

Serve with warm naan and yogurt.
Curry can be made 2 days ahead. Curry pastes vary in heat, so adjust amount to suit your taste.
Okra, also known as bamia or lady fingers, is a green, ridged, oblong pod with a furry skin. Native to Africa, this vegetable is used in Indian, Middle-Eastern and southern US cooking, and often serves as a thickener in stews. If okra is unavailable, use trimmed green beans or quartered patty-pan squash.

curried lamb puffs with cucumber raita

1 tablespoon vegetable oil
1 small brown onion (80g), chopped finely
2.5cm (1 inch) piece fresh ginger (10g), grated
1 clove garlic, grated
1 tablespoon curry powder
155g (5 ounces) minced (ground) lamb
⅓ cup (80ml) coconut cream
¼ cup (60ml) water
90g (3 ounces) pumpkin, chopped finely
¼ cup (30g) frozen peas
¼ cup finely chopped fresh coriander (cilantro)
2 sheets ready-rolled puff pastry, thawed
1 egg
CUCUMBER RAITA
1 lebanese cucumber (130g), peeled,
  grated coarsely
½ cup (140g) greek-style yogurt
½ teaspoon ground cumin
1 tablespoon finely chopped fresh mint

1 Heat oil in large frying pan, add onion, ginger, garlic and curry powder; cook, stirring, until onion softens. Add lamb; cook, stirring, until browned. Add coconut cream and the water; bring to the boil, add pumpkin. Simmer, uncovered, about 15 minutes or until pumpkin is tender and liquid is almost evaporated. Remove from heat; stir in peas and coriander, season to taste. Cool.

2 Meanwhile, make cucumber raita.
3 Preheat oven to 200°C/400°F.
4 Roll both sheets of puff pastry on floured surface to 30cm (12 inch) square. Trim edges. Cut each pastry sheet into 16 squares. Drop rounded teaspoons of lamb mixture onto each pastry square. Brush edges of pastry with egg; fold pastry diagonally over filling to make a triangle; press edges with fork to seal. Repeat with remaining pastry and lamb mixture.
5 Place triangles on baking (parchment) paper-lined oven trays. Bake about 15 minutes or until puffs are browned lightly.
6 Serve puffs with cucumber raita.
cucumber raita Squeeze excess liquid from cucumber; combine in medium bowl with remaining ingredients, season to taste.
prep + cook time 1 hour 10 minutes **makes** 32
nutritional count per puff 4.1g total fat
(1g saturated fat); 263kJ (63 cal);
4.5g carbohydrate; 2g protein; 0.4g fibre

We used jap pumpkin in this recipe, but any type will do.
Curry puffs can be made a month ahead; open freeze on trays then transfer to an airtight container or plastic bag. Cook from frozen as above.

baked lamb and sage crêpes

1 medium brown onion (150g), chopped finely
2 cloves garlic, chopped finely
3 rindless bacon slices (240g), chopped coarsely
500g (1 pound) minced (ground) lamb
½ cup (125ml) dry red wine
2 tablespoons tomato paste
½ cup (75g) seeded black olives
2 tablespoons finely shredded fresh sage
1¼ cups (310ml) bottled tomato pasta sauce
1 cup (100g) pizza cheese
SAGE CRÊPE BATTER
1½ cups (375ml) milk
30g (1 ounce) butter
2 eggs
1 cup (150g) plain (all-purpose) flour
1 tablespoon finely chopped fresh sage

1 Make sage crêpe batter.
2 Heat large oiled frying pan, add onion, garlic and bacon; cook, stirring, until onion softens. Add lamb; cook, stirring, until browned. Stir in wine and paste; bring to the boil. Reduce heat; simmer, uncovered, stirring occasionally, about 20 minutes or until sauce thickens. Remove from heat; stir in olives and sage.
3 Pour ¼-cup crêpe batter into heated oiled frying pan (base measures 15cm/6 inches); cook until bubbles begin to appear on surface. Turn crêpe, cook until browned lightly; transfer to a plate. Repeat with remaining batter to make eight crêpes.

4 Preheat oven to 220°C/425°F.
5 Place one crêpe on a board; spread ½ cup lamb mixture across centre of crêpe. Roll crêpe tightly to enclose filling; place, seam-side down, in shallow 20cm x 30cm (8 inch x 12 inch) ovenproof dish. Repeat with remaining crêpes and mince mixture. Pour over pasta sauce; sprinkle with cheese. Bake, covered, 15 minutes; uncover, bake about 5 minutes or until browned lightly.
sage crêpe batter Heat milk and butter in small saucepan until butter is melted; cool. Whisk eggs into milk mixture. Sift flour into medium bowl; stir in sage. Gradually whisk milk mixture into flour mixture until batter is smooth. Cover batter; stand 1 hour. The consistency should be like thin pouring cream; if not, add a little more milk.

prep + cook time 1 hour 10 minutes (+ standing)
serves 4
nutritional count per serving 39.6g total fat (19.7g saturated fat); 3386kJ (810 cal); 48.6g carbohydrate; 57.4g protein; 4.6g fibre

Serve with a green salad.
Leftover bolognese sauce can be used in place of the lamb mixture.
We used a thin tomato pasta sauce, also known as sugo or passata, which contains only tomatoes and onion.

spiced lamb with rice and lentils

1½ cups (300g) basmati rice
625g (1¼ pounds) minced (ground) lamb
15g (½ ounce) butter
1 medium brown onion (150g), sliced thinly
2.5cm (1 inch) piece fresh ginger (10g),
  chopped finely
2 cloves garlic, chopped finely
6 cardamom pods, bruised
1 cinnamon stick
½ cup (100g) red lentils
2½ cups (625ml) chicken stock
½ cup (80g) sultanas (golden raisins)
¼ cup (35g) slivered almonds, roasted
½ cup loosely packed fresh mint leaves
1½ cups (420g) greek-style yogurt

1 Rinse rice under cold water until water runs clear; drain.
2 Heat large oiled frying pan, add lamb; cook, stirring, until browned. Remove from pan; drain pan.
3 Heat butter in same pan, add onion, ginger and garlic; cook, stirring, until onion softens. Add cardamom and cinnamon; cook, stirring, until fragrant.
4 Return lamb to pan with rice, lentils and stock; bring to the boil. Reduce heat, simmer, covered tightly, 10 minutes. Add sultanas; cover, simmer 5 minutes.
5 Remove rice mixture from heat, remove lid, cover rice with a clean tea towel; stand 5 minutes.
6 Fluff rice with fork, sprinkle with nuts and mint; serve with yogurt.

prep + cook time 35 minutes **serves** 6
nutritional count per serving 19g total fat
(8.2g saturated fat); 2383kJ (570 cal);
61.8g carbohydrate; 35.1g protein; 4.5g fibre

lamb and chorizo rissoles

750g (1½ pounds) minced (ground) lamb
2 chorizo sausages (340g), chopped coarsely
1 small red onion (100g), chopped finely
¼ cup finely chopped fresh flat-leaf parsley
2 teaspoons finely grated lemon rind
2 teaspoons smoked paprika
2 tablespoons olive oil
ROAST CAPSICUM AND CAPER SALAD
3 medium red capsicums (bell peppers) (600g)
1 tablespoon olive oil
1 small red onion (100g), sliced thinly
1 cup loosely packed fresh flat-leaf parsley leaves
1 tablespoon rinsed, drained baby capers
1 tablespoon red wine vinegar

1   Combine lamb, sausages, onion, parsley, rind and paprika in large bowl. Shape mixture into 8 rissoles, place on tray, cover; refrigerate 1 hour.
2   Make roast capsicum and caper salad.

3   Heat oil in large frying pan; cook rissoles, in two batches, about 10 minutes or until browned both sides and cooked through. Drain on absorbent paper.
4   Serve rissoles with salad.
roast capsicum and caper salad Preheat oven to 200°C/400°F. Place capsicums on oven tray, drizzle with oil; roast about 30 minutes, turning occasionally, or until skins blacken. Place capsicums in bowl, cover, cool. Peel capsicums, discard stems and seeds. Thinly slice capsicum; combine in bowl with remaining ingredients, season to taste.

prep + cook time 1 hour 15 minutes (+ refrigeration)
serves 4
nutritional count per serving 57.7g total fat (19.8g saturated fat); 3252kJ (778 cal); 7.9g carbohydrate; 56.9g protein; 2.7g fibre

Capsicums can be replaced with roasted capsicums available from supermarkets and delicatessens.
Add green salad leaves to the salad, if you like.
Uncooked rissoles can be frozen for up to three months; thaw before cooking.

harira

1 cup (200g) dried chickpeas
1 tablespoon olive oil
2 medium red onions (340g), chopped coarsely
2 medium red capsicums (bell peppers) (400g),
  chopped coarsely
4 cloves garlic, chopped coarsely
4 cups (1 litre) chicken stock
400g (13 ounces) canned chopped tomatoes
2 cups (500ml) water
1 tablespoon fresh thyme leaves
½ cup (100g) french-style green lentils
2 tablespoons lemon juice
1 teaspoon ground cinnamon
½ cup loosely packed fresh coriander
  (cilantro) leaves
SPICED MEATBALLS
625g (1¼ pounds) minced (ground) lamb
1 small brown onion (80g), chopped finely
2 cloves garlic, chopped finely
2cm piece fresh ginger (10g), grated
1 tablespoon finely chopped fresh coriander (cilantro)
½ teaspoon ground cinnamon
1 tablespoon olive oil

1 Place chickpeas in medium bowl, cover with water; stand overnight, drain. Rinse under cold water; drain.
2 Heat oil in large heavy-based saucepan, add onion, capsicum and garlic; cook, stirring, until vegetables soften. Add chickpeas, stock, undrained tomatoes, the water and thyme; bring to the boil. Reduce heat; simmer, covered 15 minutes.
3 Add lentils to pan; simmer, covered, about 30 minutes or until chickpeas and lentils are tender, season to taste.
4 Meanwhile, make spiced meatballs.
5 Add meatballs to simmering soup; stir in juice and cinnamon. Serve soup sprinkled with coriander.
spiced meatballs Combine lamb, onion, garlic, ginger, coriander and cinnamon in medium bowl. Roll tablespoons of mixture into balls; place on tray. Heat oil in large frying pan; cook meatballs until browned all over and cooked through.
prep + cook time 1 hour 10 minutes (+ standing)
serves 6
nutritional count per serving 19.6g total fat
(6.3g saturated fat); 1881kJ (450 cal);
28g carbohydrate; 35.6g protein; 9.8g fibre

Serve with crusty bread.
French-style green lentils are related to the famous French lentils du puy; these green-blue, tiny lentils have a nutty, earthy flavour and a hardy nature that allows them to be rapidly cooked without disintegrating. Also known as australian, bondi or matilda lentils.

lamb and corn quesadillas

1 medium red onion (170g), chopped finely
2 cloves garlic, chopped finely
1 teaspoon dried chilli flakes
1 tablespoon ground coriander
3 teaspoons ground cumin
750g (1½ pounds) minced (ground) lamb
1 corn cob (400g)
2 tablespoons tomato paste
2 cups coarsely chopped fresh coriander
  (cilantro) leaves
12 flour tortillas
2 cups (220g) coarsely grated cheddar cheese
GUACAMOLE
2 small avocados (400g), mashed coarsely
2 tablespoons lime juice
½ small red onion (50g), chopped finely
½ teaspoon dried chilli flakes

1 Make guacamole.
2 Heat large oiled frying pan, add onion and garlic; cook, stirring, until soft. Add spices; cook, stirring, until fragrant. Add lamb; cook, stirring, until browned.

3 Meanwhile remove kernels from corn.
4 Add tomato paste and corn to lamb mixture, stirring until corn is softened. Remove from heat; stir in coriander, season to taste.
5 To make quesadillas, heat medium frying pan, place one tortilla in pan; sprinkle over about 2 tablespoons cheese, top with ½ cup lamb mixture, sprinkle with more cheese. Place another tortilla on top, pressing down gently. Cook both sides until browned lightly and cheese is melted. Repeat with remaining tortillas, cheese and lamb mixture.
6 Cut quesadillas into wedges; serve with guacamole.
guacamole Combine ingredients in small bowl; season to taste.
prep + cook time 50 minutes **serves** 6
nutritional count per serving 41.9g total fat (16.9g saturated fat); 3227kJ (772 cal); 51.5g carbohydrate; 45g protein; 5.5g fibre

Quesadillas can be made in a flat sandwich press.
You can use 1 cup frozen or drained canned corn kernels instead of the fresh corn, if you prefer.

lamb and olive balls with anchovy aïoli

625g (1¼ pounds) minced (ground) lamb
1 medium red onion (170g), chopped finely
2 cloves garlic, chopped finely
4 drained anchovy fillets, chopped finely
2 teaspoons finely grated lemon rind
1 tablespoon finely chopped fresh thyme
2 tablespoons finely chopped fresh flat-leaf parsley
30 large pimiento-stuffed green olives (150g)
½ cup (75g) plain (all-purpose) flour
2 eggs, beaten lightly
2 cups (340g) polenta
vegetable oil, for shallow-frying
ANCHOVY AÏOLI
2 egg yolks
2 drained anchovy fillets
1 clove garlic, chopped coarsely
1 teaspoon finely grated lemon rind
1 tablespoon lemon juice
¾ cup (180ml) olive oil

1 Combine lamb, onion, garlic, anchovy, rind and herbs in large bowl. Roll a tablespoon of mixture into a ball around each olive; place on tray. Refrigerate 1 hour.
2 Meanwhile, make anchovy aïoli.
3 Toss balls in flour; shake away excess. Dip balls in egg, then roll in polenta; place on tray. Refrigerate 1 hour.
4 Heat oil in medium frying pan; shallow-fry meatballs, in batches, until cooked. Drain on absorbent paper.
5 Serve meatballs with aïoli and lemon wedges.
anchovy aïoli Blend or process egg yolks, anchovy, garlic, rind and juice until smooth. With motor operating, gradually add oil in a thin stream; blend until thick, season to taste. Drizzle with extra olive oil, to serve.
prep + cook time 50 minutes (+ refrigeration)
makes 30
nutritional count per ball 13.9g total fat (2.7g saturated fat); 815kJ (195 cal); 11.1g carbohydrate; 6.4g protein; 0.6g fibre

For a quick version of anchovy aïoli, stir finely chopped anchovies, garlic, rind and juice into your favourite mayonnaise.

kibbeh with tomato and pomegranate salad

1 cup (160g) fine burghul
2 cups (500ml) water
625g (1¼ pounds) minced (ground) lamb
1 medium brown onion (150g), chopped finely
½ teaspoon each ground cinnamon, cumin
   and coriander
3 pieces preserved lemon rind
1 large pomegranate (430g)
3 medium ripe tomatoes (450g), chopped coarsely
2 cups loosely packed fresh mint leaves
2 cups loosely packed fresh flat-leaf parsley leaves
2 tablespoons olive oil
1 tablespoon lemon juice
125g (4 ounces) fetta cheese, crumbled coarsely

1 Combine burghul and the water in medium bowl; stand 2 hours. Drain.

2 Preheat oven to 180°C/350°F. Oil 20cm x 30cm (8 inch x 12 inch) pan.

3 To make kibbeh, combine burghul with lamb, onion and spices; season. Spread lamb mixture into pan; smooth top. Bake about 25 minutes or until cooked through.

4 Meanwhile, remove and discard flesh from preserved lemons. Rinse rind well then slice thinly. Remove seeds from pomegranate.

5 Combine rind in medium bowl with tomato and herbs. Drizzle with combined oil and lemon juice.

6 Cut kibbeh into six squares, cut each square into two triangles, place on plates; top with tomato mixture, sprinkle with fetta and pomegranate seeds.

prep + cook time 40 minutes (+ standing) **serves** 6
nutritional count per serving 22g total fat
(8.9g saturated fat); 1843kJ (441 cal);
25.2g carbohydrate; 63.6g protein; 10.4g fibre

To remove the seeds from pomegranate, cut it in half crossways and hold each half cut-side down over a bowl. Hit the outside skin of the fruit sharply with a wooden spoon – as hard as you can – the seeds should fall out – if they don't, dig them out with a teaspoon.
Burghul is made from whole wheat kernels, which are steamed, dried and toasted before cracking into several distinct sizes, so they develop a rich, nutty flavour. Because it is already partially cooked, burghul only requires minimal cooking. Cracked wheat, on the other hand, is raw whole wheat.

lamb, chilli and garlic penne

Cook 375g (12 ounces) penne pasta in large saucepan of boiling water until tender. Drain, return to pan. Meanwhile, squeeze meat from 6 thick lamb sausages (560g). Heat oiled large frying pan, add 1 thinly sliced fresh small red thai (serrano) chilli and 3 finely chopped garlic cloves; stir until fragrant. Add lamb; stir until browned. Add lamb mixture to pasta with 45g (1½ ounces) baby rocket (arugula) leaves and 185g (6 ounces) halved cherry tomatoes; toss to combine, season to taste. Serve sprinkled with shaved parmesan cheese.

prep + cook time 15 minutes **serves** 4
nutritional count per serving 26.6g total fat (11g saturated fat); 3060kJ (732 cal); 74.1g carbohydrate; 45.9g protein; 5.1g fibre

lamb dogs with mint and almond butter

Combine ⅓ cup (95g) almond butter, ½ cup finely chopped fresh mint leaves and 1 finely chopped fresh green chilli in a bowl; stir in ¼ cup hot water. Grill or barbecue 4 thin lamb sausages (325g) until cooked through. Halve 4 long soft bread rolls lengthways, spread with mint and almond butter; top with sausages. Divide 1 thinly sliced lebanese cucumber (130g) and ½ cup of fresh mint leaves between rolls.

prep + cook time 20 minutes **makes** 4
nutritional count per serving 29.6g total fat (8.6g saturated fat); 2479kJ (593 cal); 45.2g carbohydrate; 33.3g protein; 6.9g fibre
Almond butter, also known as almond spread, can be bought from health-food shops – it is similar to peanut butter.

honey-mustard chipolatas

Preheat oven to 200°C/400°F. Twist 12 chipolata sausages (570g) in half then cut to make 24 mini chipolatas; place in baking dish. Combine ⅓ cup honey with 2 tablespoons wholegrain mustard and 3 teaspoons hot english mustard; drizzle over sausages. Roast about 30 minutes, stirring occasionally, until cooked through. Serve chipolatas drizzled with any mustard and honey glaze left in the baking dish.

prep + cook time 40 minutes **makes** 24
nutritional count per chipolata 4.3g total fat (1.8g saturated fat); 355kJ (85 cal); 5.5g carbohydrate; 6g protein; 0.2g fibre

moroccan sausage rolls

Preheat oven to 220°C/425°F. Cut six rectangles from each of 2 sheets ready-rolled puff pastry. Spread ½ cup harissa paste evenly over the 12 pastry rectangles. Using 12 chipolata sausages (570g), place one on each pastry rectangle, roll up pastry to enclose chipolata; brush ends with egg to seal. Place, seam-side-down, on baking-paper-covered oven trays. Brush pastry with egg; cut slits in tops of rolls, sprinkle with about 1 tablespoon dukkah. Bake rolls about 30 minutes or until cooked through.
prep + cook time 45 minutes **makes** 12
nutritional count per roll 15.5g total fat (4.7g saturated fat); 974kJ (233 cal); 13.2g carbohydrate; 10.3g protein; 0.6g fibre

oven-baked lamb sausages with tomatoes and beans

Preheat oven to 200°/400°F. Cook 8 thick lamb sausages (700g) in flameproof dish on stove top, until browned all over. Add 2 coarsely chopped large zucchini (300g), 1 coarsely chopped medium red capsicum (bell pepper) (200g) and 400g (13 ounces) canned diced tomatoes. Cover dish, roast about 40 minutes or until sausages are cooked through. Uncover dish, add 400g (13 ounces) canned rinsed and drained cannellini beans; roast about 10 minutes or until beans are heated through. Remove dish from oven; slice sausages thickly. Serve sausages with tomatoes and beans; sprinkle with ½ cup loosely packed fresh basil leaves.
prep + cook time 1 hour **serves** 4
nutritional count per serving 32.6g total fat (13.5g saturated fat); 2529kJ (605 cal); 24.1g carbohydrate; 50.1g protein; 8.2g fibre

rosemary lamb sausages with buttermilk mash

Preheat oven 200°C/400°F. Remove rosemary leaves from all but the tops of 8 stems of rosemary; discard or reserve rosemary leaves for another use. Use rosemary stems to skewer 8 thick lamb sausages (700g); place on baking-paper-covered oven tray. Roast sausages about 25 minutes, turning occasionally, until cooked through. Meanwhile, boil, steam or microwave 4 medium potatoes (800g) until tender; drain. Place in medium bowl; mash with 1 cup buttermilk until smooth; season to taste. Combine 1 coarsely grated medium red apple (150g) with 315g (10 ounces) sauerkraut in a medium saucepan; stir over low heat until hot. Serve sausages with mash and sauerkraut.
prep + cook time 35 minutes **serves** 4
nutritional count per serving 33.3g total fat (14.3g saturated fat); 2855kJ (683 cal); 41.5g carbohydrate; 51.2g protein; 6.5g fibre

pork & veal

pork pie

375g (12 ounces) minced (ground) pork
315g (10 ounces) lean boneless pork, chopped coarsely
4 rindless bacon slices (260g), chopped finely
1 tablespoon each finely chopped fresh flat-leaf parsley and sage
½ teaspoon each ground nutmeg, allspice and black pepper
1 drained anchovy fillet, chopped finely
1 egg, beaten lightly
HOT WATER PASTRY
¾ cup (180ml) water
90g (3 ounces) butter, chopped coarsely
2⅔ cups (400g) plain (all-purpose) flour
JELLY
1 cup (250ml) chicken stock
1 cup (250ml) water
5 teaspoons powdered gelatine

1 Make hot water pastry and jelly.
2 Preheat oven to 220°C/425°F. Grease 20cm (8 inch) round spring form tin.
3 Combine pork, bacon, herbs, spices and anchovy in large bowl.

4 Roll two-thirds of the pastry on floured surface until large enough to line base and side of tin. Ease pastry into tin, press into side; trim edge, make sure there are no cracks in the pastry. Place tin on oven tray. Fill with pork mixture then pour over ⅓ cup jelly; brush edge of pastry with egg. Roll remaining pastry to cover filling; pinch edge to seal. Cut 2.5cm (1 inch) circle from top of pie, discard circle; brush pastry top with egg.
5 Bake pie 30 minutes. Reduce heat to 200°C/400°F. Bake a further 1¼ hours. Cool.
6 Using a funnel, pour remaining slightly warmed jelly slowly into hole in pie. Cover, refrigerate overnight. Cut pie into wedges to serve.

hot water pastry Bring water and butter to the boil in small saucepan then add to processor with the flour; process until ingredients come together. Knead dough on floured surface until smooth. Cover; refrigerate 30 minutes.
jelly Bring chicken stock and the water to the boil in small saucepan. Remove from heat; stir in gelatine until dissolved.
prep + cook time 2 hours 20 minutes (+ cooling & refrigeration) **serves** 10
nutritional count per serving 15.1g total fat (7.6g saturated fat); 1513kJ (362 cal); 29.2g carbohydrate; 26.4g protein; 1.5g fibre

Use as much of the jelly mixture as the pie will hold – keep topping it up slowly to allow time for the jelly to settle through the meat mixture.

pork, veal and eggplant stew

¼ cup (60ml) olive oil
1 medium brown onion (150g), chopped finely
2 stalks celery (300g), trimmed, chopped finely
1 medium carrot (120g), chopped finely
2 cloves garlic, crushed
315g (10 ounces) minced (ground) pork
315g (10 ounces) minced (ground) veal
1 tablespoon finely chopped fresh rosemary
1 cinnamon stick
2 cloves
1 cup (250ml) dry white wine
400g (13 ounces) canned diced tomatoes
1 cup (250ml) chicken stock
1 medium eggplant (300g), chopped coarsely
1 tablespoon coarse cooking (kosher) salt
500g (1 pound) tagliatelle pasta

1 Heat 1 tablespoon of the oil in large frying pan, add onion, celery, carrot and garlic; cook, stirring, until onion softens.
2 Add minces, rosemary, cinnamon and cloves to pan; cook, stirring, until browned. Add wine; simmer, uncovered, until liquid has reduced by a third. Add undrained tomatoes and stock; bring to the boil. Reduce heat; simmer, covered, 30 minutes.
3 Meanwhile, place eggplant in colander, sprinkle with salt; stand 20 minutes. Rinse eggplant; drain, pat dry. Heat remaining oil in large frying pan; stir eggplant until browned. Add eggplant to meat mixture; simmer, uncovered, 15 minutes. Season to taste.
4 Cook pasta in large saucepan of boiling water until tender; drain.
5 Serve pasta with meat sauce.
prep + cook time 1 hour 10 minutes **serves** 6
nutritional count per serving 17.9g total fat (4.4g saturated fat); 2466kJ (590 cal); 63.3g carbohydrate; 33.6g protein; 6.2g fibre

Some butchers sell a pork and veal mixture, this is fine to use here – buy 625g (1¼ pounds).

pork and veal meatballs with fresh tomato sauce

2 tablespoons olive oil
1 small brown onion (80g), chopped finely
1 clove garlic, crushed
315g (10 ounces) minced (ground) pork
315g (10 ounces) minced (ground) veal
1 cup (70g) stale breadcrumbs
2 teaspoons finely grated lemon rind
2 tablespoons roasted pine nuts, chopped coarsely
½ cup (40g) finely grated parmesan cheese
2 teaspoons finely chopped fresh oregano
2 tablespoons finely chopped fresh flat-leaf parsley
1 teaspoon sweet paprika
1 egg
500g (1 pound) spaghetti
TOMATO SAUCE
1 teaspoon olive oil
1 clove garlic, chopped finely
6 medium tomatoes (900g), chopped coarsely
2 tablespoons fresh oregano, chopped finely

1 Heat 2 teaspoons of the oil in small frying pan, add onion and garlic; cook, stirring, until soft. Cool.
2 Combine onion mixture with minces, breadcrumbs, rind, nuts, cheese, herbs, paprika and egg in large bowl; season. Roll tablespoons of mixture into balls; place on tray, refrigerate 30 minutes.
3 Make tomato sauce.
4 Heat remaining oil in large frying pan; cook meatballs, until browned all over. Add meatballs to tomato sauce; simmer, uncovered, 10 minutes or until cooked through.
5 Meanwhile, cook spaghetti in large saucepan of boiling water until tender; drain.
6 Serve spaghetti topped with meatballs, tomato sauce and some extra parmesan cheese.

tomato sauce Heat oil in large saucepan; cook garlic, stirring, until fragrant. Add tomatoes and oregano to pan; bring to the boil. Reduce heat, simmer, uncovered, about 15 minutes or until mixture has thickened. Season to taste.

prep + cook time 1 hour (+ refrigeration) **serves** 6
nutritional count per serving 22.1g total fat (5.9g saturated fat); 2692kJ (644 cal); 68.8g carbohydrate; 39g protein; 5.8g fibre

Some butchers sell a pork and veal mixture, this is fine to use here – buy 625g (1¼ pounds).

sang choy bow

15g (½ ounce) dried shiitake mushrooms
⅔ cup (160ml) boiling water
1 tablespoon peanut oil
625g (1¼ pounds) minced (ground) pork
2 cloves garlic, crushed
2.5cm (1 inch) piece fresh ginger (10g), grated
1 can (227g) water chestnuts, rinsed, drained,
  chopped finely
½ cup (125ml) chinese rice wine
1 tablespoon white sugar
1 tablespoon oyster sauce
1 tablespoon light soy sauce
1 cup (80g) bean sprouts
4 green onions, sliced thinly
8 large iceberg lettuce leaves, trimmed

1 Combine mushrooms and the water in heatproof medium bowl; stand 5 minutes. Drain mushrooms, reserve liquid; chop mushrooms finely.
2 Meanwhile, heat oil in wok; stir-fry pork, garlic and ginger until browned.
3 Add chestnuts, mushrooms, rice wine and sugar to wok; stir-fry 1 minute. Add sauces and reserved liquid; stir-fry until liquid is reduced to a syrup consistency. Remove from heat. Add sprouts and onion; toss to combine.
4 Divide pork mixture between lettuce leaves.
prep + cook time 25 minutes **serves** 4
nutritional count per serving 16g total fat (4.9g saturated fat); 1421kJ (340 cal); 10.2g carbohydrate; 33.1g protein; 2.5g fibre

pork balls with soy and lime dipping sauce

1 tablespoon sesame seeds, toasted
1 clove garlic, crushed
2.5cm (1 inch) piece fresh ginger (10g), grated
1 green onion, sliced thinly
1 tablespoon sesame oil
1 tablespoon japanese soy sauce
1 fresh small red thai (serrano) chilli, sliced thinly
500g (1 pound) minced (ground) pork
vegetable oil, for shallow-frying
SOY AND LIME DIPPING SAUCE
1 tablespoon japanese soy sauce
2 teaspoons mirin
1 teaspoon rice vinegar
1 teaspoon finely grated lime rind
1½ tablespoons lime juice
1 green onion, chopped finely
1 fresh small red chilli, sliced thinly

1 Combine seeds, garlic, ginger, onion, oil, sauce, chilli and pork in medium bowl. Roll tablespoons of mixture into balls; place on tray, refrigerate 30 minutes.
2 Make soy and lime dipping sauce.
3 Heat oil in large frying pan; cook balls until cooked through, drain on absorbent paper.
4 Serve balls with dipping sauce.
soy and lime dipping sauce Combine ingredients in small bowl.

prep + cook time 30 minutes (+ refrigeration)
makes 20
nutritional count per ball 6.2g total fat (1.2g saturated fat); 322kJ (77 cal); 0.2g carbohydrate; 5.3g protein; 0.1g fibre

pork and veal ravioli with burnt butter sauce

1 tablespoon olive oil
1 shallot (25g), chopped finely
1 clove garlic, crushed
60g (2 ounces) prosciutto, chopped finely
125g (4 ounces) minced (ground) pork
125g (4 ounces) minced (ground) veal
⅓ cup (80ml) dry white wine
⅓ cup (80ml) chicken stock
2 tablespoons roasted pine nuts, chopped coarsely
1 tablespoon finely chopped fresh marjoram leaves
2 egg yolks
1 egg, beaten lightly
8 fresh pasta sheets (375g)
BURNT BUTTER SAUCE
90g (3 ounces) butter, chopped coarsely
12 fresh sage leaves
1 tablespoon fresh marjoram leaves
2 tablespoons lemon juice

1 Heat oil in large frying pan, add shallot; cook, stirring, until soft. Add garlic, prosciutto, pork and veal; cook, stirring, until browned.
2 Add wine and stock; simmer, uncovered, until liquid is reduced by half. Stir in nuts and marjoram; season to taste. Remove from heat; stand 5 minutes. Stir in egg yolks; cool.

3 To make ravioli, brush one pasta sheet lightly with beaten egg. Place teaspoons of filling, about 2.5cm (1 inch) apart, in two rows along the length of the pasta sheet. Top with second pasta sheet; smooth pasta over filling to remove air and enclose filling. Cut between filling into squares leaving 1cm (½ inch) border on each side; place on lightly floured tray. Repeat with two more pasta sheets.
4 Drop ravioli into large saucepan of boiling water, return to the boil, simmer 2 minutes or until cooked through. Drain; return ravioli to pan to keep warm.
5 Meanwhile, make burnt butter sauce.
6 Toss burnt butter sauce through ravioli. Serve with flaked parmesan cheese, if you like.
burnt butter sauce Heat butter in large frying pan over high heat until bubbling and starting to brown; add herbs. Cook 30 seconds then remove from heat; stir in juice.
prep + cook time 1 hour (+ refrigeration) **serves** 6
nutritional count per serving 25.7g total fat (11.1g saturated fat); 2094kJ (501 cal); 43.5g carbohydrate; 20.7g protein; 2.4g fibre

Some butchers sell a pork and veal mixture, this is fine to use here – buy 250g (8 ounces).

pork, olive and egg empanadas

1 tablespoon olive oil
1 medium brown onion (150g), chopped finely
½ teaspoon each ground cumin, cinnamon and smoked paprika
¼ teaspoon each ground nutmeg and cloves
375g (12 ounces) minced (ground) pork
2 hard-boiled eggs, coarsely grated
⅓ cup (40g) seeded black olives, chopped finely
6 sheets ready-rolled shortcrust pastry
1 egg, beaten lightly

1 Heat oil in large frying pan, add onion; cook, stirring, until soft. Add spices and pork; cook, stirring, until browned. Cool.
2 Stir hard-boiled eggs and olives into pork mixture, season to taste.
3 Preheat oven to 200°C/400°F. Oil two oven trays.
4 To make empanadas, cut 24 x 12cm (5 inch) rounds from pastry sheet. Drop heaped tablespoons of filling onto rounds; brush edges with beaten egg. Fold rounds in half to enclose filling; pinch edges to seal.
5 Place empanadas on oven trays with sealed edge upright; brush with egg. Bake, about 25 minutes or until browned lightly. Serve with lemon wedges.
prep + cook time 1 hour **makes** 24
nutritional count per empanada 14g total fat (6.7g saturated fat); 961kJ (230 cal); 19.2g carbohydrate; 6.7g protein; 0.9g fibre

farmhouse terrine with spinach

1 bunch spinach (500g), trimmed
15g (½ ounce) butter
1 small brown onion (80g), chopped finely
4 rindless bacon slices (260g), chopped finely
2 cloves garlic, crushed
1 teaspoon fresh thyme leaves
¼ cup (60ml) brandy
1 egg, beaten lightly
500g (1 pound) minced (ground) pork
375g (12 ounces) minced (ground) veal
¼ cup finely chopped fresh flat-leaf parsley
1 tablespoon finely shredded fresh sage
½ teaspoon ground allspice

1 Preheat oven to 180°C/350°F.
2 Drop spinach leaves into medium saucepan of boiling water; return to the boil, drain. Drop spinach into large bowl of iced water; drain. Dry spinach leaves flat on absorbent paper.
3 Line 12cm x 25cm (5 inch x 10 inch) (1.5-litre/6-cup) loaf pan with spinach leaves, leaving 5cm (2 inch) overhang on long sides of pan.
4 Heat butter in medium frying pan; add onion, bacon, garlic and thyme; cook, stirring, until onion softens. Add brandy; simmer, uncovered, until liquid is reduced by about one-third. Transfer to large bowl; cool.
5 Add remaining ingredients to onion mixture; season. Press mixture into pan; fold spinach over meat mixture.
6 Cover pan with foil, place pan in medium baking dish with enough boiling water to come halfway up side of pan. Cook about 1¼ hours or until terrine is firm and juices run clear.
7 Refrigerate overnight before turning out.

prep + cook time 1 hour 40 minutes (+ refrigeration)
serves 8
nutritional count per serving 14.4g total fat (5.7g saturated fat); 1166kJ (279 cal); 1.2g carbohydrate; 31.6g protein; 2g fibre

Some butchers sell a pork and veal mixture, this is fine to use here – buy 875g (1¾ pounds).

oven-baked stuffed capsicums

1 tablespoon olive oil
1 large brown onion (200g), chopped finely
2 cloves garlic, crushed
250g (8 ounces) minced (ground) pork
250g (8 ounces) minced (ground) veal
2 teaspoons fresh thyme leaves
1 cup (250ml) tomato pasta sauce
1 cup (250ml) chicken stock
½ cup (100g) white long-grain rice, rinsed, drained
¼ cup finely chopped fresh flat-leaf parsley
4 medium red capsicums (bell peppers) (800g)
¼ cup (15g) stale breadcrumbs
¼ cup (20g) finely grated parmesan cheese
1 teaspoon finely grated lemon rind

1 Preheat oven to 200°C/400°F.
2 Heat oil in large frying pan, add onion and garlic; cook, stirring, until onion softens. Add pork and veal and half the thyme; cook, stirring, until browned. Add sauce, stock, rice and parsley; bring to the boil. Reduce heat; simmer, uncovered, about 15 minutes or until rice is almost tender, stirring occasionally, season to taste.
3 Meanwhile, oil small baking dish. Cut tops from capsicums, reserve as lids. Scoop out seeds and membranes. Fill capsicums with mince mixture; stand upright in baking dish.
4 Combine breadcrumbs, cheese, rind and remaining thyme in small bowl. Sprinkle over filling; place capsicum tops in baking dish. Bake capsicums, uncovered, about 1 hour or until rice is soft. Top with lids to serve.

prep + cook time 1 hour 35 minutes **serves** 4
nutritional count per serving 16.2g total fat (5.3g saturated fat); 1827kJ (437 cal); 36.4g carbohydrate; 34.2g protein; 3.8g fibre

Some butchers sell a pork and veal mixture, this is fine to use here – buy 500g (1 pound).

squid with pork and pistachios

2 cloves garlic, crushed
⅔ cup (90g) roasted unsalted shelled pistachios, chopped coarsely
2 tablespoons finely chopped preserved lemon rind
2 teaspoons sumac
1 teaspoon ground ginger
625g (1¼ pounds) minced (ground) pork
⅓ cup each coarsely chopped fresh flat-leaf parsley and coriander (cilantro)
1 fresh long green chilli, chopped finely
1 egg, beaten lightly
2 tablespoons olive oil
8 medium squid tubes (480g)
PARSLEY SALAD
2 cups loosely packed fresh flat-leaf parsley leaves
1 teaspoon finely grated lemon rind
1 tablespoon olive oil
2 teaspoons lemon juice

1 Preheat oven to 200°C/400°F.
2 Combine garlic, nuts, rind, spices, pork, herbs, chilli, egg and half the oil in medium bowl; season.
3 Place mixture into piping bag; fill squid tubes with mixture. Secure openings with toothpicks.
4 Heat remaining oil in medium flameproof dish, add squid tubes; cook until browned all over. Transfer dish to oven; roast about 15 minutes or until cooked through. Stand 5 minutes then slice each tube into four pieces.
5 Meanwhile, make parsley salad.
6 Serve squid with parsley salad and lemon wedges.
parsley salad Combine ingredients in medium bowl; season to taste.

prep + cook time 35 minutes **serves** 4
nutritional count per serving 38.9g total fat (8.2g saturated fat); 2529kJ (605 cal); 4g carbohydrate; 58.3g protein; 4.5g fibre

Preserved lemon can be bought in delis and some supermarkets. Remove and discard the flesh then wash and dry the rind before chopping.

pork and broad bean pilaf with pumpkin

500g (1 pound) fresh broad (fava) beans, shelled
2 tablespoons olive oil
250g (8 ounces) minced (ground) pork
250g (8 ounces) minced (ground) veal
1 medium red onion (170g), chopped finely
2 cloves garlic, crushed
625g (1¼ pounds) piece pumpkin, trimmed,
  chopped coarsely
1½ cups (300g) basmati rice
2 teaspoons ground allspice
3 cups (750ml) chicken stock
2 tablespoons lemon juice
1 cup coarsely chopped fresh coriander (cilantro)

1 Drop beans into medium saucepan of boiling water. Return to the boil; drain, then drop into medium bowl of iced water; drain. Remove outer skin from beans.

2 Heat half the oil in large frying pan, add minces; cook, stirring, until browned. Remove from pan.

3 Heat remaining oil in same pan, add onion and garlic; cook, stirring, until browned lightly. Add pumpkin, cook, stirring, 1 minute. Return mince to pan with rice and allspice; stir in stock, bring to the boil. Reduce heat; simmer, covered tightly, about 12 minutes or until rice is tender, season to taste.

4 Remove from heat; stir in beans, juice and coriander. Serve with lemon wedges and yogurt.

prep + cook time 50 minutes **serves** 4
nutritional count per serving 19.8g total fat (5.5g saturated fat); 2650kJ (634 cal); 72.1g carbohydrate; 38.7g protein; 5.63g fibre

Some butchers sell a pork and veal mixture, this is fine to use here – buy 500g (1 pound).

pork and pistachio dolmades

1 tablespoon olive oil
1 medium brown onion (150g), chopped finely
2 cloves garlic, crushed
185g (6 ounces) minced (ground) pork
½ cup (100g) white long-grain rice
½ cup (60g) roasted unsalted pistachios,
  chopped coarsely
2 teaspoons finely grated lemon rind
1 tablespoon finely shredded fresh mint
40 large grape vine leaves in brine
1 litre (4 cups) chicken stock
⅓ cup (80ml) lemon juice

1 Heat oil in medium frying pan, add onion and garlic; cook, stirring, until onion softens. Combine onion mixture in medium bowl with pork, rice, nuts, rind and mint; season.
2 Rinse, drain and dry vine leaves. Place a vine leaf, smooth side down, on bench. Place heaped teaspoons of filling across the base of each vine leaf, fold base and sides over filling; roll up to enclose filling. Line large heavy-based saucepan with 5 vine leaves; place rolls, close together, seam-side down, on leaves.
3 Add stock and juice to pan; cover with remaining vine leaves. Place a plate on top of the leaves to keep rolls immersed in liquid. Bring to the boil; reduce heat, simmer 45 minutes. Remove from heat; cool.
prep + cook time 1 hour 20 minutes **makes** 30
nutritional count per serving 2.2g total fat
(0.4g saturated fat); 192kJ (46 cal);
3.6g carbohydrate; 2.6g protein; 0.7g fibre

pork, mushroom and sage lasagne

1 tablespoon olive oil
1 small brown onion (80g), chopped finely
2 cloves garlic, crushed
1 chorizo sausage (170g), chopped finely
315g (10 ounces) minced (ground) pork
315g (10 ounces) minced (ground) veal
½ cup (125ml) marsala
½ cup (125ml) chicken stock
6 large sheets dried lasagne (250g)
¾ cup (60g) finely grated parmesan cheese
12 fresh sage leaves
MUSHROOM MIXTURE
20g (¾ ounce) dried porcini mushrooms
½ cup (125ml) boiling water
15g (½ ounce) butter
1 small brown onion (80g), chopped finely
1 clove garlic, crushed
185g (6 ounces) button mushrooms, sliced thinly
1 tablespoon coarsely shredded fresh sage
WHITE SAUCE
60g (2 ounces) butter
⅓ cup (50g) plain (all-purpose) flour
1.25 litres (5 cups) hot milk

1 Make mushroom mixture and white sauce.
2 Reserve a third of the white sauce; combine remaining sauce with mushroom mixture.
3 Preheat oven to 200°C/400°F.
4 Heat oil in large frying pan, add onion, garlic and chorizo; cook, stirring, until onion softens. Add minces; cook, stirring, until browned. Add marsala, stock and reserved porcini liquid; bring to the boil. Reduce heat, simmer, uncovered, until reduced by about a third.

5 Oil ovenproof dish (2-litre/8-cup). Place two lasagne sheets in base of dish. Top with half the mince mixture then half the mushroom mixture; sprinkle with ¼ cup of the cheese. Repeat layering, finishing with remaining two pasta sheets. Spread with white sauce; top with sage, sprinkle with remaining cheese.
6 Bake, uncovered, about 40 minutes or until browned lightly. Stand 5 minutes before serving.
mushroom mixture Combine porcini with the boiling water in medium heatproof bowl for 5 minutes. Drain, reserve liquid (for meat mixture); chop porcini finely. Heat butter in large frying pan, add onion and garlic; cook, stirring, until onion softens. Add button mushrooms and porcini; cook, stirring, until mushrooms are browned. Add sage; season to taste.
white sauce Melt butter in medium saucepan, add flour; cook, stirring, until mixture bubbles. Gradually stir in milk; cook, stirring, until mixture boils and thickens. Simmer, stirring, 2 minutes; season to taste.
prep + cook time 1 hour 10 minutes **serves** 6
nutritional count per serving 41.2g total fat (20.7g saturated fat); 3106kJ (743 cal); 41.8g carbohydrate; 44.5g protein; 2.8g fibre

Porcini, dried Italian mushrooms, are available from delicatessens, gourmet food stores and some supermarkets.
Some butchers sell a pork and veal mixture, this is fine to use here – buy 625g (1¼ pounds).

pork and prawn toasts

2 cloves garlic, crushed
1 shallot (25g), chopped finely
2 tablespoons coarsely chopped fresh
    coriander (cilantro)
1 egg
155g (5 ounces) minced (ground) pork
90g (3 ounces) prawn meat, chopped coarsely
1 teaspoon white sugar
2 teaspoons fish sauce
8 slices white bread (360g), crusts removed
vegetable oil, for shallow-frying

1 Blend or process garlic, shallot, coriander, egg, pork, prawn, sugar and sauce until smooth.
2 Spread pork mixture evenly over bread slices; cut each slice into 4 triangles.
3 Heat oil in large frying pan; shallow-fry triangles, meat-side-down, in batches, turning once, until cooked through. Drain on absorbent paper. Serve immediately.

prep + cook time 30 minutes **makes** 32
nutritional count per serving 3.2g total fat
(0.5g saturated fat); 259kJ (62 cal);
5.2g carbohydrate; 2.8g protein; 0.4g fibre

If buying prawns in the shell, you will need to buy about 185g (6 ounces) uncooked prawns.

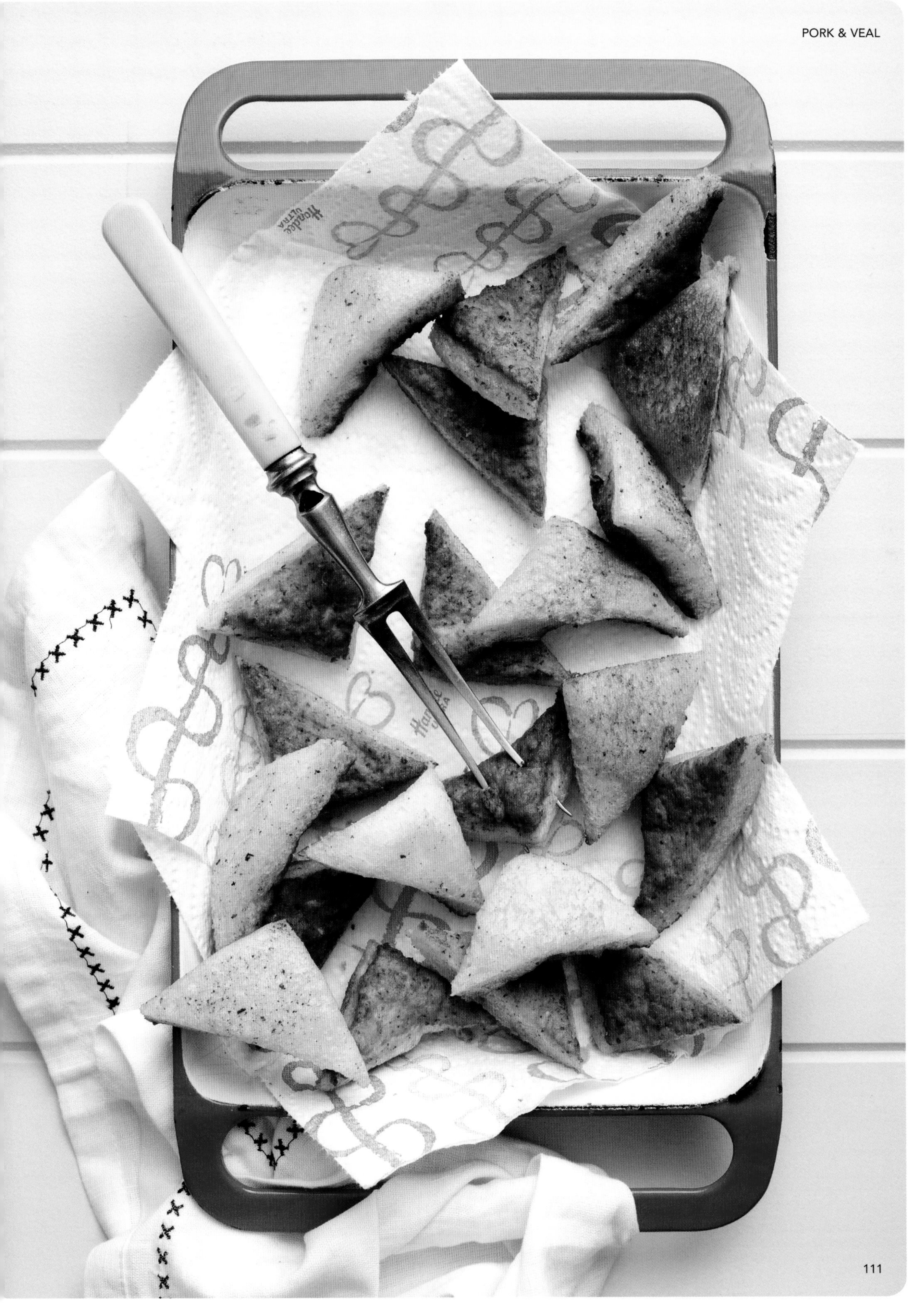

sausage and cannellini bean bake

Preheat oven to 220°C/425°F. Cook 8 thick pork sausages (1kg) in heated oiled medium flameproof dish, on stove top, until browned. Remove from dish. Meanwhile, thinly slice 2 medium brown onions (300g); finely chop 2 teaspoons fresh thyme. Cook onions in same heated dish, stirring, until browned. Return sausages to dish with 400g (13 ounces) canned undrained diced tomatoes, half the thyme and 420g (13 ounces) canned rinsed, drained cannellini beans. Tear 3 slices white bread into small pieces; sprinkle over sausages with remaining thyme. Bake, in oven, about 15 minutes or until heated through.

prep + cook time 25 minutes **serves** 4

nutritional count per serving 54.9g total fat (21.7g saturated fat); 3398kJ (813 cal); 37.7g carbohydrate; 38g protein; 10.9g fibre

bangers and mash with red wine gravy

Boil, steam or microwave 5 coarsely chopped medium potatoes (1kg) until tender, drain. Mash potato in large bowl with ⅔ cup milk and 30g (1 ounce) butter; season to taste. Meanwhile, cook 8 thick pork sausages (1kg) in heated oiled large frying pan until browned; remove from pan. Add 2 thinly sliced large brown onions (400g) to same pan; cook, stirring, until soft. Return sausages to pan with ¾ cup dry red wine; bring to the boil. Reduce heat, simmer, uncovered, until liquid is reduced by a third. Serve sausages with red wine gravy and mashed potato.

prep + cook time 20 minutes **serves** 4

nutritional count per serving 61.3g total fat (26.7g saturated fat); 3804kJ (910 cal); 42.9g carbohydrate; 36.8g protein; 7.8g fibre

toad in the hole

Preheat oven to 220°C/425°F. Combine 2 lightly beaten eggs, 1 cup milk and 1 teaspoon finely chopped fresh rosemary in medium jug. Sift 1 cup plain (all-purpose) flour into medium bowl, make well in centre; whisk in egg mixture until smooth. Cover, stand 30 minutes. Meanwhile, divide 1 tablespoon vegetable oil between 6 holes of texas muffin pan (¾ cup/180ml). Divide 6 small thin pork sausages (520g) among pan holes; bake about 15 minutes or until browned. Pour batter over sausages while muffin pan is hot. Bake about 15 minutes or until puffed and browned.

prep + cook time 40 minutes (+ standing) **makes** 6

nutritional count per piece 26g total fat (9.8g saturated fat); 1647kJ (394 cal); 22.8g carbohydrate; 16.7g protein; 2.1g fibre

sausages with braised lentils

Add 1½ cups french-style green lentils to medium saucepan of cold water; bring to the boil. Reduce heat; simmer, uncovered, about 20 minutes or until tender, drain. Meanwhile, cook 8 thick pork sausages (1kg) in heated oiled large frying pan until cooked through. Remove sausages from pan; drain excess fat from pan. Cook 1 finely chopped shallot in same pan until soft. Add lentils; cook, stirring, 2 minutes. Remove from heat; stir in ¼ cup lemon juice, 1 tablespoon olive oil and ¾ cup coarsely chopped fresh flat-leaf parsley, season to taste. Slice sausages; serve with lentil mixture and lemon wedges.

prep + cook time 30 minutes **serves** 4
nutritional count per serving 61.5g total fat (23.4g saturated fat); 3795kJ (908 cal); 35.6g carbohydrate; 47.6g protein; 13.6g fibre

pork sausage and broccoli stir-fry

Cut 250g (8 ounces) broccoli into small florets. Thinly slice 1 fresh large red chilli. Chop 90g (3 ounces) garlic chives coarsely. Cook 6 thick pork sausages (700g) in medium saucepan of boiling water about 12 minutes or until cooked through; drain, cool then slice sausages. Pour boiling water over 1 packet (450g) hokkien noodles in heatproof bowl, separate with fork; drain. Heat oiled wok; stir-fry sausages with ¼ cup XO or oyster sauce and the sliced chilli; add broccoli, stir-fry 1 minute or until tender, adding a little water if necessary. Add noodles; stir-fry until hot. Stir in garlic chives before serving.

prep + cook time 20 minutes **serves** 4
nutritional count per serving 40.5g total fat (16g saturated fat); 3302kJ (790 cal); 68g carbohydrate; 35g protein; 7g fibre

sausages with mushy peas and potato cake

Place 3 peeled potatoes (900g) in medium saucepan of cold water. Bring to the boil; boil, covered, 5 minutes; drain. Cool 5 minutes. Bring ⅔ cup chicken stock to the boil in medium saucepan; add 3 cups frozen minted baby peas (360g); simmer, uncovered, until tender. Blend undrained peas until almost smooth. Meanwhile, cook 8 thick pork sausages (1kg) in heated oiled large frying pan until cooked. Remove from pan; cover to keep warm. Wipe pan with absorbent paper. Coarsely grate potato into medium bowl. Add 2 thinly sliced green onions (scallions); season. Heat 15g (½ ounce) butter in pan. Shape potato into 4 patties; cook until browned both sides and heated through. Serve sausages with potato cakes and mushy peas.

prep + cook time 25 minutes **serves** 4
nutritional count per serving 59.3g total fat (24.6g saturated fat); 3628kJ (868 cal); 38.8g carbohydrate; 40.4g protein; 11.6g fibre

Glossary

ANCHOVY small silvery green fish of the herring family – are not sardines. Fresh anchovies have a mild, slightly oily flavour. Preserved anchovies are typically packed in salt and oil; they can be extremely salty, and can be soaked in cold water or milk to draw out the excess salt.

BABY ASIAN SALAD MIX (mixed baby asian greens) a packaged mix of baby buk choy, choy sum, gai lan and water spinach. Available from Asian food stores and most supermarkets.

BAKING PAPER (parchment paper or baking parchment) a silicone-coated paper primarily used for lining baking pans and oven trays so biscuits and cakes won't stick making removal easy.

BEANS

broad also known as fava, windsor and horse beans; available dried, fresh and frozen. Fresh and frozen forms should be peeled twice, discarding both the outer long green pod and the beige-green tough inner shell.

cannellini small white bean similar in appearance and flavour to other white beans: haricot, navy or great northern beans, any of which can be used.

green also known as french or string beans, this long thin fresh bean is consumed in its entirety once cooked.

kidney medium-size red bean, slightly floury in texture yet sweet in flavour; sold dried or canned.

snake long (about 40cm), thin, round, fresh green beans; Asian in origin, with a taste similar to green beans. Are also called yard-long beans because of their (pre-metric) length. If snake beans are unavailable, use green beans.

sprouts also known as bean shoots; tender new growths of beans and seeds germinated for consumption as sprouts. The most readily available are mung bean, soya bean, alfalfa and snow pea sprouts.

white in this book, some recipes may call for 'white beans', a generic term we use for canned or dried cannellini, haricot, navy or great northern beans any of which can be used.

BREADCRUMBS

packaged fine-textured, crunchy, purchased white breadcrumbs.

stale one- or two-day-old bread made into crumbs by blending or processing.

BUK CHOY also known as bok choy, pak choi, chinese white cabbage or chinese chard; has a fresh, mild mustard taste. Use both stems and leaves. A commonly used asian green.

BURGHUL made from whole wheat kernels, which are steamed, dried and toasted before cracking into several distinct sizes; has a rich, nutty flavour. Because it is already partially cooked, burghul only requires minimal cooking. Not the same as cracked wheat, which is raw whole wheat.

BUTTER use salted or unsalted (sweet) butter; 125g is equal to one stick (4 ounces) of butter.

BUTTERMILK originally the term given to the slightly sour liquid left after butter was churned from cream, today it is made similarly to yogurt. Sold alongside fresh milk products in supermarkets. Despite the implication of its name, it is low in fat.

CAPERS the grey-green buds of a warm climate (usually Mediterranean) shrub, sold either dried and salted or pickled in a vinegar brine. Baby capers, those picked early, are very small, fuller-flavoured and more expensive than the full-sized ones. Capers must be rinsed well before using.

CAPSICUM also known as bell pepper or, simply, pepper. They come in many colours: red, green, yellow, orange and purplish-black. Discard seeds and membranes before use.

CHEESE

bocconcini a walnut-sized, baby mozzarella. Is a delicate, semi-soft, white cheese traditionally made from buffalo milk. Spoils rapidly so must be kept under refrigeration, in brine, for 1 or 2 days at most.

cheddar a semi-hard, cow's-milk cheese. Has a slightly crumbly texture if properly matured.

fetta a crumbly goat's- or sheep's-milk cheese with a sharp salty taste.

mozzarella a soft, spun-curd cheese. It has a low melting point and an elastic texture when heated; is used to add texture rather than flavour.

parmesan also known as parmigiano; a hard, grainy cow's-milk cheese.

pizza a blend of grated mozzarella, cheddar and parmesan cheeses.

ricotta the name for this soft, white, cow's-milk cheese roughly translates as 'cooked again'. It's made from whey, a by-product of other cheese-making, to which fresh milk and acid are added. Ricotta is a sweet, moist cheese with a slightly grainy texture.

swiss a generic name for a variety of cheeses originating in Switzerland, among them emmentaler and gruyere.

CHICKPEAS also called garbanzos, channa or hummus; round, sandy-coloured legume.

CHILLIES available in many different types and sizes. Use rubber gloves when seeding and chopping fresh chillies as they can burn your skin. Removing seeds and membranes lessens the heat level.

CHINESE COOKING WINE also known as shao hsing or chinese rice wine; made from fermented rice, wheat, sugar and salt with a 13.5 per cent alcohol content. Inexpensive and found in Asian food shops; if you can't find it, replace with mirin or sherry.

CHIPOLATA SAUSAGES also known as 'little fingers'; highly spiced, coarse-textured, usually beef, sausage although they may also be made with chicken.

CORIANDER both the stems and roots of coriander are used in cooking; wash well before using. Also available ground or as seeds; these should not be substituted for fresh coriander as the tastes are completely different.

CREAM

cream we used fresh cream, unless otherwise stated. Also known as pure cream and pouring cream; has no additives unlike commercially thickened cream. Minimum fat content 35%.

sour a thick cultured soured cream. Minimum fat content 35%.

CURRY PASTES some recipes in this book call for commercially prepared pastes of various strength and flavours. Use whichever one you feel suits your spice-level tolerance best.

powder a blend of ground spices; consists of dried chilli, cinnamon, cumin, coriander, fennel, fenugreek, mace, cardamom and turmeric. Can be mild or hot.

red probably the most popular curry paste; a hot blend of different flavours including red chilli, garlic, shallot, lemon grass, salt, galangal, shrimp paste, kaffir lime peel, coriander, cumin, paprika. It is milder than the hotter thai green curry paste.

DUKKAH is an Egyptian spice blend made of roasted nuts and aromatic spices. It is available from Middle-Eastern food stores, specialty spice stores and some supermarkets.

FLOUR
plain an all-purpose flour made from wheat.

self-raising plain flour sifted with baking powder in the proportion of 1 cup plain flour to 2 teaspoons baking powder.

GARAM MASALA a blend of spices based on cardamom, cinnamon, coriander, cloves, fennel and cumin, roasted and ground together. Black pepper and chilli can be added for a hotter version.

HARISSA a Moroccan sauce or paste made from dried chillies, cumin, garlic, oil and caraway seeds. It is available in Middle-Eastern food shops and major supermarkets.

KECAP MANIS see sauces.

LENTILS (red, brown, yellow) dried pulses often identified by and named after their colour.

french-style green lentils related to the famous french lentils du puy; these green-blue, tiny lentils have a nutty, earthy flavour and a hardy nature that allows them to be rapidly cooked without disintegrating. Are also known as australian, bondi or matilda lentils.

MIRIN this Japanese, champagne-coloured cooking wine is made of glutinous rice and alcohol, and used expressly for cooking. Should not be confused with sake.

MUSHROOMS
button small, cultivated white mushrooms with a mild flavour.

flat large, flat mushrooms with a rich earthy flavour, ideal for filling and barbecuing. They are sometimes misnamed field mushrooms, which are wild mushrooms.

swiss brown also known as cremini or roman; light to dark brown mushrooms with full-bodied flavour. Button or cup mushrooms can be substituted.

MUSTARD
american-style bright yellow in colour, a sweet mustard containing mustard seeds, sugar, salt, spices and garlic. Serve with hamburgers.

dijon a pale brown, distinctively flavoured, fairly mild french mustard.

english an extremely hot powdered mustard containing ground mustard seeds (both black or brown and yellow-white), wheat flour and turmeric. Also available in a milder, less hot, version.

wholegrain also known as seeded. A French-style coarse-grain mustard made from crushed mustard seeds and dijon-style french mustard.

OKRA also known as bamia or lady fingers, a green, ridged, oblong pod with a furry skin. Native to Africa, this vegetable is used in Indian, Middle-Eastern and southern USA cooking.

OLIVES
black have a richer and more mellow flavour than the green ones and are softer in texture. Sold either plain or in a piquant marinade.

pimiento-stuffed green a green olive with a lively, briny bitterness containing a morsel of capsicum, which adds a flash of colour.

PAPRIKA ground, dried sweet red capsicum (bell pepper); there are many types available, including mild, sweet, hot and smoked.

PITTA also known as lebanese bread. This wheat-flour pocket bread is sold in large, flat pieces that separate into two thin rounds. Also available in small thick pieces called pocket pitta.

PIZZA BASES pre-packaged for home-made pizzas. They come in a variety of sizes (snack or family) and thicknesses (thin and crispy, or thick), and taste great with your favourite pizza toppings.

POLENTA also known as cornmeal; a flour-like cereal made of ground corn (maize). Also the name of the dish made from it.

POMEGRANATE to remove the seeds from a pomegranate, cut it in half crossways and hold each half, cut-side down, over a bowl. Hit the outside skin of the fruit sharply with a wooden spoon – as hard as you can – the seeds should fall out – if they don't, dig them out with a teaspoon.

PRAWNS also known as shrimp.

PRESERVED LEMON RIND a North African specialty; lemons are quartered and preserved in salt and lemon juice or water. To use, remove and discard pulp, squeeze juice from rind, rinse rind well; slice thinly. Sold in jars or singly by delicatessens; once opened, store under refrigeration.

PROSCIUTTO a kind of unsmoked Italian ham; salted, air-cured and aged, it is usually eaten uncooked.

RICE
arborio small, round-grain rice, well-suited to absorb a large amount of liquid; especially suitable for risottos.

basmati a white, fragrant long-grained rice. Wash several times before cooking.

jasmine fragrant long-grained rice; white rice can be substituted, but will not taste the same.

long-grain elongated grain, remains separate when cooked; most popular steaming rice in Asia.

SALT, COARSE COOKING is coarser than table salt, but not as large-flaked as sea salt: it is sold packaged in bags in most supermarkets.

SAUCES
barbecue a spicy, tomato-based sauce used to marinate or baste, or as a condiment.

black bean a Chinese sauce made from fermented soya beans, spices, water and wheat flour.

char siu a Chinese barbecue sauce made from fermented soya bean paste, sugar, water, salt, honey, soy sauce, malt syrup and spices. It can be found at most supermarkets.

cranberry a packaged product made of cranberries cooked in sugar syrup.

fish also called nam pla or nuoc nam; made from pulverised salted fermented fish, most often anchovies. Has a pungent smell and strong taste, so use according to your taste.

hoisin a thick, sweet and spicy Chinese sauce made from salted fermented soya beans, onions and garlic; used as a marinade or baste.

oyster Asian in origin, this rich, brown sauce is made from oysters and their brine, cooked with salt and soy sauce, and thickened with starches.

plum a thick, sweet and sour dipping sauce made from plums, vinegar, sugar, chillies and spices.

soy also known as sieu, is made from fermented soya beans. Several variations are available in most supermarkets and Asian food stores. We use a mild Japanese variety in our recipes; possibly the best table soy and the one to choose if you only want one variety.

japanese soy an all-purpose low-sodium soy sauce made with more wheat content than its Chinese counterparts; fermented in barrels then aged.

kecap manis a dark, thick sweet soy sauce. Depending on the brand, the soy's sweetness is derived from the addition of either molasses or palm sugar when brewed.

light soy a pale, fairly thin, but salty-tasting sauce; used in dishes in which the natural colour of the ingredients is to be maintained. Don't confuse with salt-reduced or low-sodium soy sauces.

sweet and sour a blend of tomatoes, onions, capsicum, carrots, pineapple and selected spices.

sweet chilli a comparatively mild, Thai-style sauce made from red chillies, sugar, garlic and vinegar.

tomato also known as ketchup or catsup; a flavoured condiment made from tomatoes, vinegar and spices.

tomato pasta made from a blend of tomatoes, herbs and spices.

worcestershire a dark-coloured condiment made from garlic, soy sauce, tamarind, onions, molasses, lime, anchovies, vinegar and seasonings. Available in most supermarkets.

xo a spicy seafood sauce made from dried fish and shrimp and cooked with chilli, onion, garlic and oil. It is available from Asian food stores.

SAUSAGE minced meat seasoned with salt and spices, mixed with cereal and packed into casings. Also known as snags or bangers.

SAUSAGE MINCE finely chopped and seasoned meat, usually pork.

SQUID a type of mollusc; also known as calamari. Buy squid hoods to make preparation easier.

STOCK cans, bottles, tetra packs, cubes, powder or concentrated liquid can be used. As a guide, 1 teaspoon of stock powder or 1 small crumbled stock cube or 1 portion stock concentrate mixed with 1 cup (250ml) water will give a fairly strong stock. Be aware of the salt and fat content of stocks.

SUGAR
caster also known as superfine or finely granulated table sugar.
light brown a soft, fine sugar retaining molasses for its colour and flavour. Dark brown sugar may be substituted.
palm sugar also known as nam tan pip, jaggery, jawa or gula melaka; made from the sap of the sugar palm tree. Light brown to black in colour and usually sold in rock-hard cakes; the sugar of choice in Indian and most South-East Asian cooking. Substitute it with brown sugar, if unavailable.
white a coarse, granulated table sugar, also known as crystal sugar.

SUGAR SNAP PEAS also known as honey snap peas; fresh small pea that can be eaten whole, pod and all, similarly to snow peas.

SULTANAS dried grapes, also known as golden raisins.

SUMAC a purple-red, astringent spice ground from berries growing on shrubs that flourish wild around the Mediterranean; adds a tart, lemony flavour to foods.

TACO SEASONING MIX found in most supermarkets; is meant to duplicate the taste of a Mexican sauce made from oregano, cumin, chillies and other spices.

TAGLIATELLE PASTA long, flat strips, slightly narrower and thinner than fettuccine, which can be substituted.

TAMARIND CONCENTRATE the commercial distillation of tamarind pulp into a condensed paste. Used straight from the container, with no soaking or straining required; can be diluted with water according to taste. Found in Asian food stores and many larger supermarkets.

TURMERIC, GROUND also known as kamin; known for the golden colour it imparts to the dishes of which it's a part.

VINEGAR
balsamic originally from Modena, Italy and made from the juice of Trebbiano grapes; it is a deep rich brown colour with a sweet and sour flavour.
brown malt made from fermented malt and beech shavings.
red wine based on fermented red wine.
rice a colourless vinegar made from fermented rice and flavoured with sugar and salt. Is also known as seasoned rice vinegar.
white wine made from a blend of white wines.

WATER CHESTNUTS resemble a chestnut in appearance, hence the English name. They are small brown tubers with a crisp, white, nutty-tasting flesh. Their crunchy texture is best experienced fresh, however, canned water chestnuts are more easily obtained and can be kept about a month, once opened, under refrigeration.

WATERCRESS also known as winter rocket, is a dark-green, slightly peppery leaf. Highly perishable, so must be used as soon as possible after purchase.

WONTON WRAPPERS also known as wonton skins; made of flour, eggs and water, they come in varying thicknesses. Sold packaged in large amounts and found in the refrigerated section of supermarkets and Asian grocery stores; gow gee or spring roll pastry sheets can be substituted.

YOGURT we use plain unflavoured yogurt unless otherwise directed.

ZUCCHINI also known as courgette; belongs to the squash family.

Conversion Chart

MEASURES

One Australian metric measuring cup holds approximately 250ml; one Australian metric tablespoon holds 20ml; one Australian metric teaspoon holds 5ml.

The difference between one country's measuring cups and another's is within a two- or three-teaspoon variance, and will not affect your cooking results. North America, New Zealand and the United Kingdom use a 15ml tablespoon.

All cup and spoon measurements are level. The most accurate way of measuring dry ingredients is to weigh them. When measuring liquids, use a clear glass or plastic jug with the metric markings.

We use large eggs with an average weight of 60g.

DRY MEASURES

METRIC	IMPERIAL
15g	½oz
30g	1oz
60g	2oz
90g	3oz
125g	4oz (¼lb)
155g	5oz
185g	6oz
220g	7oz
250g	8oz (½lb)
280g	9oz
315g	10oz
345g	11oz
375g	12oz (¾lb)
410g	13oz
440g	14oz
470g	15oz
500g	16oz (1lb)
750g	24oz (1½lb)
1kg	32oz (2lb)

LIQUID MEASURES

METRIC	IMPERIAL
30ml	1 fluid oz
60ml	2 fluid oz
100ml	3 fluid oz
125ml	4 fluid oz
150ml	5 fluid oz
190ml	6 fluid oz
250ml	8 fluid oz
300ml	10 fluid oz
500ml	16 fluid oz
600ml	20 fluid oz
1000ml (1 litre)	1¾ pints

LENGTH MEASURES

METRIC	IMPERIAL
3mm	⅛in
6mm	¼in
1cm	½in
2cm	¾in
2.5cm	1in
5cm	2in
6cm	2½in
8cm	3in
10cm	4in
13cm	5in
15cm	6in
18cm	7in
20cm	8in
23cm	9in
25cm	10in
28cm	11in
30cm	12in (1ft)

OVEN TEMPERATURES

The oven temperatures in this book are for conventional ovens; if you have a fan-forced oven, decrease the temperature by 10-20 degrees.

	°C (CELSIUS)	°F (FAHRENHEIT)
Very slow	120	250
Slow	150	300
Moderately slow	160	325
Moderate	180	350
Moderately hot	200	400
Hot	220	425
Very hot	240	475

Index

Published in 2010 by ACP Books, Sydney

ACP Books are published by ACP Magazines a division of PBL Media Pty Limited

General manager Christine Whiston
Editor-in-chief Susan Tomnay
Creative director Hieu Chi Nguyen
Art director & designer Hannah Blackmore
Design assistant Sarah Holmes
Senior editor Wendy Bryant
Food director Pamela Clark
Sales & rights director Brian Cearnes
Marketing manager Bridget Cody
Senior business analyst Rebecca Varela
Circulation manager Jama Mclean
Operations manager David Scotto
Production manager Victoria Jefferys

Published by ACP Books, a division of
ACP Magazines Ltd, 54 Park St, Sydney;
GPO Box 4088, Sydney, NSW 2001.
phone (02) 9282 8618; fax (02) 9267 9438.

acpbooks@acpmagazines.com.au;
www.acpbooks.com.au

Printed by Toppan Printing Co, China.

United Kingdom Distributed by Australian Consolidated Press (UK),
phone (01604) 642 200; fax (01604) 642 300; books@acpuk.com

Title: Mince it / food director Pamela Clark.
ISBN: 978 186396 936 9 (pbk.)
Notes: Includes index.
Subjects: Mincemeat. Cookery (Meat)
Other Authors/Contributors: Clark, Pamela.
Dewey Number: 641.6362
© ACP Magazines Ltd 2010
ABN 18 053 273 546

Recipe development Rebecca Squadrito, Nicole Jennings,
Elizabeth Macri, Adelaide Harris, Dominique Gekas
Nutritional information Rebecca Squadrito

Photographer Ian Wallace
Stylist Louise Pickford
Food preparation Dom Smith
Cover Lamb, chilli and garlic penne, page 90

The publishers would like to thank the following for props used in photography:
Maxwell Williams, No Chintz Textiles and Soft Furnishings, Bourke Street Bakery.

Scanpan cookware is used in the AWW Test Kitchen.

Send recipe enquiries to:
recipeenquiries@acpmagazines.com.au